THE
FLIGHT
OF YOUR
LIFE

THE FLIGHT OF YOUR LIFE

6 PRINCIPLES TO LEVERAGE PASSION, PAIN AND PERSEVERANCE

CHARLES L. BAILEY JR., EMBA, MSES
&
YVANA HEPBURN-BAILEY, MA

The Flight of Your Life
6 Principles To Leverage Passioon, Pain and Perseverance
© 2024 by Charles L. Bailey, Jr. and Yvana Herpburn-Bailey

All rights reserved solely by the author. The author guarantees all contents are original and do not infringe upon the legal rights of any other person or work. No part of this book may be reproduced in any form without the permission of the author. The views expressed in this book are not necessarily those of the publisher.

Scriptures marked NIV are taken from the NEW INTERNATIONAL VERSION (NIV): Scripture taken from THE HOLY BIBLE, NEW INTERNATIONAL VERSION ®. Copyright© 1973, 1978, 1984, 2011 by Biblica, Inc.TM. Used by permission of Zondervan.

Unliess otherwise notes the Scriptures quoted are from the NET Bible® https://netbible.com copyright

©1996, 2019 used with permission from Biblical Studies Press, L.L.C. All rights reserved".

Printed in the United States of America.
ISBN-13: 979-8-9904645-0-6- Paperback
979-8-9904645-1-3- Dust Jacket
979-8-9904645-2-0 eBook
LCCN: 2024906653

Inspire Ink & Co Publishing
Gotha, Florida

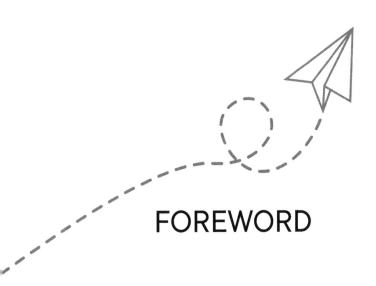

FOREWORD

Boarding an airplane can be an exhausting, entertaining, frustrating or surprisingly enlightening event. Individuals from all walks of life are traveling to one common port, yet they could be journeying to final destinations separated by thousands of miles. As I have traversed, sharing my story and mission from city to city, state to state, nationally and internationally, I have observed differences, dynamics and dichotomies with each new departure. I often find myself intrigued by the shared sense of urgency and even more so by the lack thereof regarding passengers boarding and taking their assigned seating. I vividly remember one flight in particular as I observed passengers boarding and passing by my seat in first class. Having boarded early, I took advantage of the extra time and observed the "extra baggage" that each individual boarded the plane with. I reflected on how often I have witnessed or observed each of these uniquely distinct "types."

I took notice of the "phone talker." This individual typically boards the aircraft on a business call discussing their last business meeting numbers, deals and details. The call is typically vocally energized and is often framed with, "Hey buddy, I'm boarding my flight; let's discuss details when I land." I am

THE FLIGHT OF YOUR LIFE

typically perplexed by these calls and ask why might the passenger have waited to discuss these matters while boarding the plane rather than before. Or maybe there is a deeper need for external validation that is appeased by announcing and justifying the idea that "I am someone important." I get it, sometimes we do want others to feel that we are important or want others to get the sense that we are busy and that we are always moving even when we are sitting still.

I then took notice of the passenger wearing the deepest and darkest of sunglasses. This can mean many things and in my experience it is not uncommon to assume that they may actually be a celebrity of sorts, a professional athlete or personality, as not every high-profile individual flies private. However, as a therapist I can also recognize that sunglasses may be a means of self-protection or a guard that keeps us from truly being exposed or seen. Sunglasses are often a conversation deterrent or repellent. It could also mean that the individual has had a great time, whether departing from a vacation destination or a long day of work or just wants nothing more than to get to their seat and fall asleep. Which raises the question for you and me of why we might not want to be seen and the fluctuation between our desire to be fully exposed or to be reclusive and not allow others to look beyond our eyes.

I observed the single parent or solo parent traveling with their children, trying their absolute best to multitask while navigating the attempt to not have their child disturb other passengers. I truly applaud these warriors carrying a child on one hip, a carry-on on the other and truly admire those with multiple little ones as they corral them by hands and guide the entire family to their seats. However, I respectfully consider how unimaginably exhausting the tasks must be for them as my mind forms a picture of the events that may have led up to the scheduled trip. Like modern-day superheroes, watching them single-handedly care for several little ones, managing excitement and angst is a truly cinematic experience.

Although there are many other passenger personalities, the final dynamic I observed was the "seat-switchers." Typically, a couple has the uncomfortable circumstance of negotiating with other passengers and flight attendants to propose switching seats so that they may sit together. We have all seen this and may have experienced it ourselves. How interesting it is to listen to how the courageous passenger attempts to explain how or why they were unable to purchase seats together and the brief second that is incurred where the passenger being asked could accept or reject the proposal. There are times when the response is, "I'm sorry, but I would like to keep my seat..." or "I prefer the window (or the aisle)..." or "sorry, I purchased the entire row." Of course as much as they hope, I too hope the response could be, "sure, no worries I totally understand," but the scenario is a fifty percent chance and the result is not always up to us when it requires someone else to change their seat, course or direction. We must be prepared to accept the outcome either way and ultimately our perspective of how the desired result turned out.

Taking flight is so informative and offers wise reflection. Certainly, these examples in no way can cover all of the personalities or unique circumstances of every individual. There are passengers who just want to get home or who want to get away from the pain and lack of their familiar environment. There are also those who know where they are going but have no idea or plan for where they will end up once they get to wherever "there" is. Life can take us on an unpredictable journey whether we are prepared for the departure or not. Yet, we can work on ourselves in such a way that gives us a plan of action that will help us move ourselves towards a determined destination and find peace in knowing that life does not have to be traversed alone.

THE FLIGHT OF YOUR LIFE

    We are often in our own world or forming the world we exist in through our definition and reflection of ourselves at any given moment. But in the final moments of boarding, one thing remains clear and paramount despite how we view our world or ourselves in that moment. In order for any of us to go anywhere to take flight we must all find our seat to find where we belong to understand that whatever our challenge, struggle or mindset, our actions or inactivity is playing a part and having an impact on others that can either delay or accelerate departure. Despite the unique circumstances that can impact boarding, the managing flight staff will often make an appropriate announcement, "if you're in the aisles, we ask that you quickly find your seat so we can prepare for take-off."

    Why do they make this announcement? Each flight has a set time, a unique window set for take-off which could not only be predicated by schedule alone but other external factors like wind or weather, a connecting flight needing staffing in another city or a host of other unknowns to passengers that the flight crew is aware of. Once we all have taken our seat, the final checkpoint is to ensure that the aisle is clear. The aisle is the central pathway that allows attendants and staff to meet the needs of the passengers to move quickly and safely in the case there is an emergency and to provide easy access to refreshment or relief during the flight.

    I do not have any knowledge of where you are in your current state of life, where you are heading or envision to be. You may best identify as a "phone talker" who is always about business or dedicated to giving the impression that you are. Or the "hidden figure" who is not interested in being seen, seeing others and at times not desiring to see themselves. You may actually be a single parent just trying to manage your family and maintain your sanity or someone who is looking for adventure or a way to define a new life, a new destination or a new direction. No matter which example speaks most clearly

FOREWORD

to you, I will advise you to take a moment to clear the aisles of your life, of your mind and your soul so that you can receive the push you will need to take The Flight of Your Life.

The book you are holding has personally impacted me as I read its pages and I genuinely believe that it will challenge your perspective, intellect and emotions to the extent that you allow. It will provoke new concepts and new thought as you prepare to take flight. From a clinical perspective, I can attest most of us have too many things blocking our aisles: thoughts, trauma and even trophies of past triumphs can keep us from receiving a propulsive push. We can unknowingly remain attached to people, places and things that cause delays in our departures holding or limiting our fullest potential. Have you ever heard or experienced a "failure-to-launch" in your life?

I speak not only as a clinician, a respected thought-leader or personality, but as a former NFL athlete. I continue to recall a saying that my coach used to blurt on repeat, "you think long, you think wrong." I must admit, I didn't fully comprehend the deeper meaning of this quote until the day I realized my own propensity to overthink and under-act caused many a delay in my own life. Delays in opportunities, advancement, elevation and even my personal identity. Sometimes you, I, we, can overthink or have too many ideals cluttering our aisle and we miss great opportunities to witness what God has for us next because we cannot receive anyone challenging us to take our seat and reflect on what may be given to us now.

I encourage and implore you to take advantage of this opportunity. Clear the aisles of your mind, open up the pathways for new information to be inserted and ingrained into your thinking no matter what passenger type you may be. Charles and Yvana give great insight into the importance of propulsion, practice, parameters, programming and ultimately the reprogramming of your mindset so that you can experience different and elevated outcomes.

THE FLIGHT OF YOUR LIFE

The level of your performance is determined by the level of your preparation. As you take your journey, the flight of your life, make room in your heart and mind. Reset your heart drive and your hard drive, move some things to the recycle bin and let this manual help you delete inadequate or outdated programming that is hindering your performance, fulfillment and life impact. Be receptive as you evaluate friendships, partnerships and even familial relationships. Use this manual as a means to help you question if you are experiencing right relationships and assessing whether they are limiting you or helping you to remove limitations. Serve as your own flight crew and create a sense of urgency, remove the clutter in your mindset and prepare your spirit to receive. There is a set time for your arrival so don't hesitate any longer. Take your flight manual, take your seat and take flight.

The plane can only take off once the aisle is clear and everyone is seated with their seat belts securely fastened. Do not worry you have everything you need and what you do not have, you can purchase after you land. You already have enough luggage and the trick is to travel light, so what you have now is enough for the journey. We just need you to get there. This is your time.

Destiny is waiting, but it does not wait for long. Open your mind as you dive into this life-changing book and allow each chapter to cultivate a new mindset as you're on a flight to destiny. We can only take the flight of our life once we clear the aisle for TAKE OFF.

Clear the aisle and embrace The Flight of Your Life.

Dr. Jay Barnett, DHA
Mental Health Expert /
International Speaker

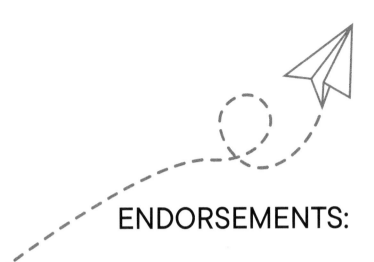

ENDORSEMENTS:

"This book is a really good look into the reality of overcoming obstacles, how to keep moving forward and upward. Now looking back as a Super Bowl Champion, it blows my mind to see how many of these principles were used with me personally to help me figure out how to get from my home town to the NFL. I am grateful for what Charles and Yvana have written in this book and I believe it will help people in every area of life, especially someone who believes that they have unique abilities to achieve more but need the right push to put their feet to action. Fly, eagles fly."

—Fletcher Cox, Super Bowl Champion, Pro Bowler, Philadelphia Eagles

"Why do some fly and others fall? Read and find out! How can we seek greatness, realize our gifts and be a light to those around us? The Flight of Your Life is an appropriate step for those who hear their calling but need the courage to respond. Coach Charles and Yvana have helped push me to great heights but more importantly they continue to build upon their legacy of propulsion through partnering with my dream every step of the way. I am glad to have them in my life and you will be too!"

—Sam Kendricks, World Champion Olympic Medalist and Soldier

THE FLIGHT OF YOUR LIFE

"Charles and Yvana have written a must-read collection of teachings that go beyond a self-help book. This book is for the dreamers looking to become doers. It is a wake-up call and a plan of action for those who have been waiting on life, to take the flight of their lives with purpose. Whether you are a new entrepreneur leading a start-up or CEO of a 7-figure business, this book will ignite purpose not just in what you do, but more importantly in who you are."

—Carolina Flores, Mom and CEO
Hi Hello

"Charles and Yvana use all of their experiences to lay out a thoughtful plan on how to move through all of life's challenges. The book is outstanding. Well worth reading."

—Joe Walker, Jr., US Olympic Committee
National Track and Field Coach of The Year

"As an organizational leader for more than two decades, I've watched a lot of very talented individuals not succeed. For many, it is because the wind in their sails are often filled with emotional exuberance. I believe Charles and Yvana offer sage advice, and a disciplined approach, for anyone desiring to succeed at their purpose in life: '…[t]hose who find purpose have elevated to a level beyond their emotion; they have found purpose in the doing despite their feelings.' Drawing from their career in the high performance training of professional and collegiate athletes this couple provides a refreshing yet challenging approach to succeeding in the doing. Worth the read. Even more, worth the consultation."

—Rick Whitted, CEO, Author and Speaker
Outgrow Your Space At Work

"After thirty years of service, I feel this is a book that every service member should be given at the moment they enter into service on how to pursue their goals in a Godly manner. Incredibly

ENDORSEMENTS:

thoughtful, unique and special gift—I am highly impressed with Charles and Yvana. While reading, I felt the love and spirit behind their efforts. This powerful book with its insights, takes you on a journey that leaves you encouraged to be all God has created you to be. Perfect landing!"

—Marcus Campbell, Ph.D., Command Sergeant Major
U.S. Army Retired

"Charles and Yvana, thank you for sharing life situations and testimonies inside this book that will help so many people!"

—Orien Watson, Sport Marketing Manager
C Spire Wireless

"The Flight of Your Life will be just below the Bible in my aresenal or reference books. Time and again it calls something to the front of my mind I needed in that moment. I challenge everyone to engage with this living and breathing work. It shines light in the nooks and crannies with the overlay of how to process and propel.

—Leah Purvis, Chief Lending Officer & Enthusiast
Greystone

"The Flight of Your Life really spoke to me most particularly in the area of knowing my worth. The principle of seeing my 'no' as my greatest 'yes' has inspired me to keep my eyes and actions toward my determined destination propelling me towards a greater purpose of helping others become better prepared for times of transition."

—Jamil Northcutt, Ph.D., SVP, Major League Soccer
CEO, Strategic Transition Advisors, LLC

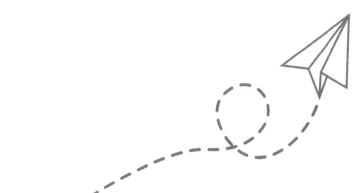

TABLE OF CONTENTS

CHAPTER 1: PREPARING FOR TAKEOFF 1
    PURPOSE BEYOND PASSION 6
    MAKE THAT CHANGE 9
    DARE TO DEFY 13
    SEAT OF SELF-DISCIPLINE 18
    THE BOARDING CALL 21

CHAPTER 2: PROPULSION VERSUS COMPULSION 27
    RELATIONSHIPS 32
    RESPONSIBILITIES 38
    REHEARSALS 45
    RUMBLINGS 51
    ROUSINGS 55

CHAPTER 3: POWER AND POTENTIAL 61
    FORCE IS KING 65

THE FLIGHT OF YOUR LIFE

    RECOVERY IS QUEEN 71
    LAWS FOR LIFE 79
    USE IT OR LOSE IT. 86
    DO NOT STOP 95

CHAPTER 4: POTENTIAL AND PROBLEMS. 103
    ATTITUDE AND LATITUDE (FREEDOM). 109
    BELONGING IS BELIEVING (FAITH). 115
    ONLY BELIEVERS BELONG (FRIENDS). 119
    FLICKER OF FIRED (FORTITUDE) 125
    FIGHT AND FLIGHT (FOCUS) 131

CHAPTER 5: PUSHING THE LIMIT 137
    BE THE BOSS 147
    "NO" YOUR WORTH 150
    LIVE THE PRE-SENT 155
    MAKE YOUR MOVE. 161
    GO THE FASTEST. 167

CHAPTER 6: PREPARED FOR IMPACT 173
    GENERATE IT. 177
    BECOME IT. 184
    REFLECT IT. 189
    LIVE IT 195
    GIVE IT 200

ABOUT THE AUTHORS 209

NEXT STEPS AND BONUS MATERIALS 211

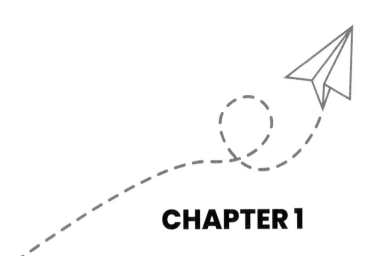

CHAPTER 1

Preparing for Takeoff

If you are still looking for your *calling* or calling it that, it may be time to stop looking and start listening. *Calling* is not something that is out in front of you; it is not something somewhere out there in some distant ethereal space. It is a mechanism intended to get you to actively turn and to propel in a direction toward a defined destination with purpose. It is that purpose in which you must choose that a calling identifies in you. Calling is by design, all around you and will continue to beckon and has been since the day of your birth. We are typically thrust into the world, pushed into it and from that moment we have been accelerating toward an unknown future. That initial push will only stop when you no longer have breath. To be honest, it is not a calling that we are after but rather to understand what is pushing us forward. It is our job to propel and to discover what propels us. It is our duty to perceive and to remove those things which may be hindering us.

Life is an irrevocable gift that cannot be returned back to sender. This gift of direction is an eternal power that moves

THE FLIGHT OF YOUR LIFE

all things and gives life to all things, like the wind that blows; you may hear it and see the impact made from it but you cannot truly know where it comes from or where it is going. It is a power that propels. In science, energy is eternal; once it has been generated it can never be destroyed. Thrust into existence by a word, it will continue along the path as it will always look to be expressed in the fullness of that potential. This gift of direction is found in every living thing; it is found within you. It is divinely directed, set in motion before you or anything existed. Power put in words propelled the cosmos and by design, will continue to provide you and everything else direction for all of eternity.

Your life—all our lives—have been given this gift of direction. The potential is intended to propel the fabric of space and time into purpose. Unfortunately despite not being capable of being destroyed, this power can be repurposed and generate momentum in a direction that was never intended. You may have sensed that you were made for more, but over time you may have been redirected through various circumstances or your own fears. You may have perceived that you were made to move culture or to move more efficiently through life and at your highest level; but, you cannot seem to place where that power has gone or fear that you are out of position to be propelled even if the power were to hit you. We are here to help re-position you and re-introduce you to purpose so that you may remove limitations and experience lift. This book is strategically designed to inspire you to be empowered, increase that power and to use it to propel yourself into the flight of your life. It is our greatest hope that this book will challenge you and *push* you above the surface to connect you with a calling and then to inspire you to propel any and everything that you come in contact with.

Yvana and I will do our best to ensure that by the end of this book, you are better prepared to take the flight of your life and that you would embrace why it is so important that you fulfill your true purpose. To do this, we are going to discuss a few familiar topics like *calling, passion, purpose* and others in a way that will move you from motivation to inspiration. There is a difference between the two. This book will combine principles from business, science, sports, relationships and our life to give clarity of your purpose beyond the calling and to identify whether you are misidentifying both. We will also push you in areas and push you to deal with areas that may be the disconnect between you and the *source* of power that will help you reach the ultimate *goal*. As we continue we ask that you open your heart and mind to challenge yourself, your current status or situation and your thinking.

By the end of this book you may feel that you are exactly where you should be—nowhere near where you would be or as far off as you allow yourself to be but either way, your life experience has always been and will forever be your call to make. The best way to look at calling is to understand its purpose. A call is a means of getting attention. The call itself neither creates forward or backward acceleration. Calling is neither a destination, passion or your purpose. In most cases a call is a disrupter of direction. It causes us to pause when our focus is to proceed. A call has both pitch and tone and depending on these, the call could mean different things. No matter, the call is only effective if it provokes action. How we respond or position ourselves to take action is entirely up to our choosing despite the consequence.

There is a marketing term that you may be familiar with: *a call to action (CTA)*. This term better illustrates our point. Every marketer knows that effective marketing impacts our behavior; it gets us to do something. It is estimated that we encounter over ten thousand unique advertisements each day. Each advertisement is aimed to stimulate action. Each carefully crafted message is vying for our attention

THE FLIGHT OF YOUR LIFE

competing for top-of-mind awareness that elicits an objective response. When done right, they are designed to influence our desires and emotions in such a way that we can no longer control them but rather, that messaging prompts us to purchase. The call is the game but it is not the goal. The goal is the purchase decision and just like calling, the purchase decision belongs only to you. What you do with your calling is up to you; it has always been.

    Whether you feel that you have experienced your calling or not has no ultimate bearing on your decision to pursue what propels you. Some things we do simply because we want to do them. There is an old saying, "people make time for the things they want to do." When we make up our minds to do something, we search for and allow almost any justification, action or energy required to complete the transaction or goal. Calling is not and will never be your goal. Your intent, energy, actions and ultimately your direction are the targets. It is our vision Yvana and I, to give you insight that will help you focus on action as it is the expression of potential, of power that can move us and others forward—upward.

*What you **do** with your calling **is** up to you; it has always been.*

    To maximize our potential and the rate at which we take action we must deliberately choose not to become distracted by every calling that we will hear along the way. This creates the *paralysis of analysis* or the overwhelming feeling that we should answer every one of them. We can become fearful that we will miss out, succumb to the pressure and come away with more than we bargained for or can handle.

A wise person once said, "never go grocery shopping when you are already hungry." You can imagine why that is not always a good idea. It is easy to go into a grocery store focused on one or two items only to leave with more than you budgeted for.

It is the same occurrence as being pressured to take advantage of a "once in a lifetime" opportunity. We already know before we commit that the only thing we can afford is to wait! Callings can shift our focus to people, places and things that do not align with our true desires or direction. If we are not diligent we can actually become controlled by every passing message and never regain or recognize that we are being pulled in every direction except the direction that we know we must go.

Whatever your situation, we want to push you to change the way you see yourself and your potential. We want to encourage you to do whatever is necessary to propel yourself and others to more. Maybe the fear of missing out has restrained you from pushing your limits. Maybe you have surrendered to distractions, or destruction of your power rather than focusing on your personal development and growth. This is the first thing necessary to be checked before you can take the flight of your life. If you are living under the mistaken belief that you will hear a calling once and for all, then you are not actually stewarding the gifts, skills, talents and abilities that you were equipped with. You are not living a life propelled; you are living one that is compelled.

The question to be answered is whether you are being pulled by every force around you or if you are actively embracing and exploiting the push from which your life was accelerated into purpose. After all, the moment you were born you were born with one. No matter who you came from or how you got here, your purpose was meant to continue the flow of the potential within you giving life and creating

THE FLIGHT OF YOUR LIFE

it and moving other lives forward to the greatest levels of living. We are going to spend our time together discussing the differences between compulsion and propulsion and how each of these can impact our desires, passions, direction, attitude and level of elevation. We are going to explore the business, science, risks and dangers of propulsion. We are going to take a deeper look into how propulsion is our purpose and how to maximize it using real-life examples and illustrations that are right before our eyes.

It is time that you prepare for departure. New levels of health, production, performance and joy are available to you. Before we proceed, it is important that you come to discern between passion and purpose. Too often we buy into believing that our purpose will be disguised in our passion. Whatever we may come to experience the greatest growth and impact in does not necessarily require that we be passionate about them. Passion is important but it is not your purpose. Passion will help you pursue your purpose vigorously. Do not worry if you do not currently feel passionate about your current status. Your new elevation rests more in your ability to generate large amounts of force in order to change your direction. Your passion is not your purpose. Your passion is propulsive. Passion will give you the ability to withstand the forces that would keep you from moving ahead. Passion will keep you from the compulsion of complacency.

PURPOSE BEYOND PASSION

Passions change, period. Culture tells us that to find passion is to find purpose. We disagree. Those who accomplish the impossible often express how persistence led them to their purpose. Passion often creates more pain than it does prosperity. Furthermore, being gifted to do a thing well does not inherently come with passion. There are many who do great things, lifesaving tasks even, who do not possess a deep passion for the task. There are more than many who are extremely passionate about things that they themselves are horrible at.

Defining our passion can be far more powerful than what we are actually best prepared to do. A passionate person can generate excitement concerning almost anything. Passion can enhance *persistence* and *perseverance*. It takes both of these to refuse the extrinsic motivation (compulsion) of failure or success. The persistent and those who persevere are those who are all-in no matter the cost. That is a totally different approach to life altogether. A person who is persistent and perseveres will no doubt find their purpose. Those who find purpose have elevated to a level beyond their emotion; they have found purpose in the *doing despite their feelings*. In other words, successful people are inspired by continual progress in every area and circle of their life; that is all they are after.

Many entrepreneurs, athletes or the successful elite have expressed that what they built was not the product of passion. Observe the wealth that athletes and celebrities of today are amassing. Almost gone are the days where athletes squander their entire salaries in their rookie year or debut. Socialites of today are building schools, giving scholarships, investing for the long term, building generational wealth and excelling in multiple avenues outside of their main skill. This is because they are playing for propulsion, not passion. They are visualizing their purpose and using passion to fuel it and not the other way around. They have become passionate about building bigger and using every opportunity to add value, to increase acceleration in others and to contribute to something greater that ultimately moves culture. No more "shut up and dribble," "shut up and stay in your lane" or "shut up and stay silent."

THE FLIGHT OF YOUR LIFE

On a much deeper note, *true* passion is what we are willing to endure in order to achieve what is possible. The cost of exposed greatness is a hefty price to pay in private. The hours, sacrifices and often pains endured can be demanding. If you cannot honestly say that you are willing to endure these in order to find your mission, vision, dream or goal, then you are not ready to take the flight of your life. In *Webster's Dictionary* the very word *passion* is defined by the ultimate sacrifice. You will find the crucifixion of Christ as a definition of what passion really is. That is the level to which we must be willing to go to ensure our life's purpose propels others forward. Everyone wants to be a diamond, yet no one wants to be cut. Lecrae said, "everyone wants freedom, but no one wants to hear 'about face.'"

Passion looks like Desmond Doss in *Hacksaw Ridge* or Waverly Woodson Jr.; we must be willing to go the extra mile even if it could cost us everything. The point made here is one of the strongest we can make. If you are serious about taking the flight of your life, it may require that you devote yourself to what it requires. It may mean losing weight, gaining weight, getting more education, earning more certifications, registering a business or competing for the promotion you feel qualified for. It may also mean losing pride, gaining courage, losing friends, opening your heart to new friends or seeking help—whatever it takes to move forward. It is all about propulsion.

Passion is not what brings a smile to our face, a tear to our eye or a rainbow over our heads and leaves rose petals after our steps. That is a scripted rom-com. True passion is sacrificial if necessary, going against the grain if necessary, going with a small circle or going alone if necessary. With all of its improbabilities, risks and dangers, life is about taking flight. That is where living truly exists.

If you have a goal that you want to achieve it is imperative to focus your faith and to consistently invest your passion into the journey and adventure. Sure, you must remain prepared for the risk without losing sight of your inspiration. This will keep you moving forward even if moving forward requires that you move laterally or on to something else. As long as you are focused on moving forward, you will find the joy of true success even if it is not monetary in nature.

> True passion is sacrificial if necessary, going against the grain if necessary, going with a small circle or going alone if necessary.

Yvana and I have survived some very hard times and challenges together over the course of our marriage but we are passionate about the journey and passionate about pushing forward. The struggles, journey and adventure push us forward even when we have suffered loss of things and even dreams. Flight can be unpredictable, it may mean being hurt by a friend, losing a job or missing the mark by a hair. Those moments are tests but they are also designed to convince us that we are still on our way to more. If you are experiencing these tests, congratulations; you are moving forward. Your job is to keep moving forward; that will eventually become all you know. Moving forward will become your passion and it will fuel your purpose.

One of our favorite songs speaks to this. The song is "Walking Shoes," performed by Mali Music. We encourage you to listen to the song if you have a few moments. As you listen, we hope that you take the courage necessary to remember that passion is not purpose, but it can be found in persistence. The first verse spoke volumes to us as we were walking what felt like such a long and lonely path in preparation for the flight of our life. It does not matter how far

THE FLIGHT OF YOUR LIFE

the trip may seem or how hard it has been. Just keep walking and you will meet the dream halfway.

MAKE THAT CHANGE

You may be excited to move forward but you must become just as excited about making progress in areas that are necessary for you to change in order to move on to your next level. Sometimes the change we need is small and others, not so small. Based upon the previous discussion of passion and purpose, if we were to ask you "how would you know that you reached your purpose?" would your answer be superficial? Would your answer be based on a moment or a mission? That is a loaded question *with* purpose. It is an explorative question into your motivational factors. It is not enough to change your thoughts. You must change your perspectives and attitudes toward what you think it means to successfully take the flight of your life.

Maybe you feel that being heralded as successful is having a lot of money or being regarded as a celebrity. Imagine that you achieve this (and you very well might have already), then what? If there is nothing more after amassing large amounts of money, obtaining the promotion, achieving entertainment or athletic accomplishments or reaching such a level of attractiveness that you lose yourself in the process, then your purpose is valueless. You have no purpose. These are all meant to be vehicles of purpose. Acquiring anything and losing self or soul is the greatest loss of life. Until you can envision an impact or express your purpose as a service to the world or someone's world, the relationship between your passion and your purpose will remain broken. There is nothing wrong with any of those things in themselves. What we are saying is that in order for these to be vehicles of your purpose, the means in which you take the flight of your life you must re-pair and re-purpose them.

Zig Ziglar expresses in his book *Born to Win* that if any element of our lives is not cared for properly or takes too much of our time, energy or focus, then our vehicle is as good as stuck. He expresses that there is a unique balance of resources that are necessary to ensure that we are on our way to the top. If any of these passions are out of balance, we can even risk moving forward but at an incredibly arduous pace and with a bumpier ride than necessary. Much like a damaged wheel or rim with one spoke too long or too short, you may be able to make a trip but it will not be a pleasant journey. It may be that the road to finding your place has been rough but rather, you are living in *self-inflicted non-sense* that has been jolting you along your way. In order to make a change, it may require that you take a stop and a good hard look on what you need to assess. This book is meant to give you the appropriate time to address what will give you the best shot at maximizing your propulsion. Having any area out of alignment is going to impede your progress and may cause further damage that can halt your ability to initiate change and accelerate toward your full destiny.

> Until you can envision an impact or express your purpose as a service to the world or someone's world, the relationship between your passion and your purpose will remain broken.

Flight, maneuverability, pivots and agility all require great amounts of force and velocity. You cannot afford to ignore the flat or damaged areas. We need every motor unit working together; we need every cylinder firing. We need every rotor and drive train working simultaneously. That may mean changing things that we are quite comfortable with.

THE FLIGHT OF YOUR LIFE

You may not like change but if you claim to be willing to do whatever it takes to maximize your purpose, then you will passionately approach positive change. Flight requires willingness and preparedness to change. It requires a defiant humility to admit that we have limited our own progress in the areas that hold us back—whether it is undervaluing our effort, health, voice, influence or impact. This is why we need revolutionary change and we must be willing to be revolutionary within ourselves.

The change we speak of is a fundamental change in the way you think and speak. You apologize. Apologize to God, yourself and anyone else you need to and then take the necessary action to change your direction. That is literally what repentance is. Do not be afraid of this word. Repentance is a highly flammable and combustible substance and it can ignite our purpose with greater zeal and fire than we have known. It is here where we actively participate in the choice to move forward. If you have felt stuck in your life—relationships, performance, achievement or personal commitments—this is how you can get your propulsive momentum back. Trust us.

One of the most empowering words often tarnished or wielded unhealthily and unhelpfully by the unguided to abuse, misinform or devalue the power of experience is so much more than that. The power in repentance ignites our freedom to change; it ignites the action of acceleration. Repentance is the act of changing the heart, mind and seat of our emotions. It is characterized by a turn into what accelerates us. Maybe that is what you have been needing to do. Jeff Henderson, master chef and author of the book *My Journey from the Streets to the Stove* recounts his story as a former drug dealer. At the height of his prime, Jeff would pocket $35,000 per week cooking and selling his product that eventually landed him a twenty-year reservation in prison.

Jeff had a gift. It was cooking, presentation and business. He had plenty of passion but had no purpose. After serving his time Jeff repented. He re-paired his mindset and re-purposed his passion. Chef Jeff is now one of the most sought-after talents in the culinary arts world. He is not only an author but an international speaker and thought leader. Jeff's story is a story of commitment and redemption, but most importantly, one of change. That is repentance.

Repentance pushes us to take responsibility for our actions today despite what we may have done or encountered yesterday. Repentance offers us a starting point to become the person we were meant to become and can. Your purpose is still waiting for you but you must accept responsibility, turn around and floor the accelerator to prepare the highest level of yourself for the flight of your life. There you will find the impact and increase what you are truly after; you will fall in love with the process and propel others.

It is not uncommon for our dreams to mistake us for someone else if we are someone else when we first meet. It is until we come back to ourselves, repent to our Creator and who we were created to be that our purpose will hide itself from us intentionally. Maybe you've put on more than a few pounds. Maybe your love for others has become cold. Maybe you haven't actually put forth the effort to earn that spot you think that you deserve on the athletic or leadership team. Maybe you haven't studied enough to increase your education to the level it needs to be to get the scholarship. Repent and make moves or continue to make excuses. Either way, it is going to require courage and a humble level of defiance or you can remain in pride, fear and denial. You must embrace repentance, defy your pride and become okay with defying limits in your life that are keeping you grounded. Make whatever change necessary and do not be satisfied simply with trying. Be satisfied with trying persistently; be defiant.

DARE TO DEFY

We want you to dream but there is a point where your dream should become what you actively pursue. You have to be daring in order to defy the odds or opposition to your determined destination. There will be plenty of people in your life who do not expect you to take steps toward anything. There will be plenty of people who hope that you do, so that they can see or help you fail. Regardless, if you dream about it, it will only come to pass to the level you are willing to do anything about it. Defying odds only happens to those who dare to do so. Release and repent from hurts, habits, hang-ups and other people that either have bound or hoped to box you in. Reintroduce yourself to your creative mind and resolve to take whatever action necessary to take your dreaming to *doing*.

Dreams are worthless if you do not have the defiant audacity to commit to the path. You may experience individuals or systems whose intent is to keep your giftedness grounded. These systems may be ultra-proficient at clipping the wings of purpose-driven individuals to keep them from taking flight or eventually taking over. Do not allow these compulsive mechanisms to distract your propulsive direction even if they come disguised in the form of positional authority. In life, there are two voices: the voice of less and the voice of more.

One of the saddest things we have observed is how quickly a fear-based compulsion can take hold in those whose job is to guide and cultivate drive in those under their tutelage. We have witnessed how student-teacher, mentor-mentee, manager-employee and pastor-parishioner relationships can quickly become contentious as God begins to reveal gifts and open doors that no man can take credit for. If you have an ability and power to change culture, inspire and move others with who you are, this may put you on the radar and make you a target. Your budding clarity of purpose, self-discovery and reconnection to what your Creator has placed within you may challenge or expose weak foundations of misappropriated authority. Do not be surprised if your preparedness for takeoff triggers a response or directive aimed to contain or remove you. If this is happening in your life, accept that your purpose is propelling you *through* this path. Purpose has a uniquely bold way of pushing us through challenges rather than taking us around them. We will discuss this resistance later.

Be willing to proceed at all costs toward your determined purpose not only for yourself but for those who are destined to see your persistence to push forward or push through. It may not be popular at first but eventually, your peers, the nation or even the world will see that your truth was *the* truth. The purpose that is within you does not need permission or authorization. If you have a dream, that is your dream. Do not throw it away on account of someone else's interpretation of your dream through their lens. Daring to defy means never giving over your divine authority or the inner soul of your purpose to anyone. You must dare to remain committed to living your purpose *on purpose*.

> Purpose has a uniquely bold way of pushing us through challenges rather than taking us around them.

Steve Harvey—world renowned comedian, host, and author—tells the story of his lesson on daring to defy. Steve was faced with the moment where his purpose could have

THE FLIGHT OF YOUR LIFE

been locked away in the hangar of someone else's hands. As a boy, Steve's class was asked to write what they wanted to become when they grew up as an assignment. Steve's paper simply said, "I want to be on TV." A side note here: children often write things that they do not truly understand but there are moments like these where we all have caught a glimpse of who we were pushed into this world to become.

Steve stood in front of the class and read what he had written on *his* paper (emphasis added). He imagined that he would receive applause and encouragement. What he received was public humiliation. His teacher scolded him in front of the class and asked, "who do you know in this class or anywhere that has been on TV?" As if to add insult to injury she accused Steve of being a smart aleck, making light of his dream and writing a note to his parents to teach him a lesson!

You too, may have felt ridiculed for believing that you could accomplish something great. You too, may have experienced the humiliation of someone who missed their once-in-a-lifetime opportunity to add a propelling push to accelerate you forward. Instead of encouraging you, they took the opportunity to belittle you, your dream and what you were given to do by God.

As you could imagine Steve's heart was broken; he was confused and now very afraid. He was sure that he would be disciplined by his parents given the perspective of his teacher. Steve was right and wrong. He was about to learn a lesson in discipline. He imagined discipline would be issued much like the way we would have expected if our teacher sent us home with an accusatory note.

Instead of punishing young Steve and compelling him to throw away what he had created (what he had been created for), Mr. Harvey had the wisdom to propel. His words give us insight into how to use propulsive techniques to keep your purpose moving forward despite the pain or ridicule. The trick is to make a maneuver that satisfies the demand of opposition without ever losing your momentum. Out of respect and honor for both Steve and Mr. Harvey, we want you to read the conversation as expressed in Steve's words:

> MR. HARVEY. What did your teacher want you to write?
>
> STEVE. I don't know. I guess she wanted me to write what the other kids were writing, things like teacher, doctor, lawyer, basketball player…
>
> MR. HARVEY. Well, that's what you're going to write. Go upstairs, take a sheet of paper and write something like that and take it to your teacher. This is what I want you to do with that other paper. You keep that paper. You put it in your drawer. Every morning, I want you to read *your* paper and every night, I want you to read *your* paper. That is *your* paper. That is *your* dream.

In the famous words of Denzel Washington in *Training Day*, the flight of your life is "chess. It ain't checkers." When someone demands that you throw in the towel, be sure to autograph it first. Decide in your mind that you will buy another one and continue forward with *your* work. When someone demands that you ball your purpose up and throw it away, shoot it and say, "for Kobe," then pull out another sheet of paper and write it in permanent marker. This is *your* determined destination. This is *your* dream. This is *your*

purpose. This is *your* paper. You are doing it because *you* love it. You are doing it because *you* are propelled by it.

Defy the compulsive temptation to let your pride or emotions be the self-destructive force that destroys your destiny or delays its arrival. Your purpose is not payback. If you are motivated to do well to hurt someone else, then you are still being compelled by venomous pride and contention. Discipline yourself, practice self-control, push forward and pursue your purpose, not payback. Feint, leave them with *their* pride. You keep working in silence until your success speaks for you.

Flying is defying. There are laws that say flight should not happen successfully. There are laws that suggest bumblebees should not be capable of flight. Pilots across our world courageously defy their feelings and logic to take flight to the skies. It matters not if there is a chance you will not reach a goal; go for it anyway. You will discover yourself and the power of propulsion along the way as you help others take flight because of having encountered you. Meanwhile, you continue to work *toward* purpose.

Daring to defy looks like working toward a master's degree although your role or function does not require one. Your coach may not require extra skill training outside of practice but that is not a reason to not put in the extra reps. Your job may not require you to expose yourself to learning other business functions but running your own business might, so wear as many hats as you can. Accept it as tuition-free training. Daring to defy limitations means intentionally working to remain free from the status quo, the minimum requirement or sacrifices necessary to achieve what is within you. That is at the core of self-discipline which is at the core of any true success. Self-discipline is the seat on the flight of your life. That seat is waiting.

SEAT OF SELF-DISCIPLINE

Self-discipline is the ability to control feelings in order to overcome hesitations and hindrances. It is the ability to pursue what we are convicted of is right despite the temptations to abort or abandon it. Each day we must decide that we are willing and determined to defy our feelings, weaknesses or what makes us feel comfortable if we are going to create the amounts of momentum that we need to reach the levels or impact that we desire. Self-discipline requires partnering with the mission. Self-discipline says that you are endowed by your Creator with a gift and a *go*. In order to truly be prepared for takeoff, you must be securely fastened into your seat and buckled in. Self-discipline says, "have faith like it is up to God and work like it is up to you." The seat of self-discipline will give you the courage to forsake whatever is not in line and attack whatever is.

To lesser minds, self-discipline can be mistaken as selfishness, self-centeredness or self-serving-ness. Self-discipline is none of these; to find self-discipline is to find success. Self-discipline is the essence of devotion. You can accomplish anything if you devote yourself to it. Respected acquaintance and performance psychologist Justin Su'a wrote it this way: "choosing to be excellent isn't for the faint of heart. When you choose that path you are choosing to be different and choosing to be different makes you unrelatable. Don't be surprised when the people that are most critical of your new lifestyle are those who are closest to you."

Self-discipline will allow you to draw from the well within you when no one supports or understands where you are trying to grow or achieve. It will keep you committed to moving forward no matter the distraction. Even when you question whether you have enough power to create the lift you need, remaining seated in self-discipline will keep you

THE FLIGHT OF YOUR LIFE

from giving up your seat and conforming to the status quo. Your seat has not been reserved for anyone else; it is reserved for you and you must be disciplined in order to see it.

On a flight to see family in my hometown of Biloxi, Mississippi for Thanksgiving, I remember looking over to another row and seeing there had been two vacant seats available. There was a middle-aged gentleman who was sitting alone and I was sitting shoulder to shoulder in my seat. I had asked the flight attendant if I could switch seats and take one of the open ones next to the gentleman. After receiving approval and reaching altitude, she kindly walked me over to the empty seats and asked the gentleman if he minded to scoot to the window and allow me to have the aisle seat. He replied nicely but firmly, "no. All of these are actually my seat. I purchased the entire row." Then he laid down and went to sleep. All of the seats were his and self-discipline will give you the confidence and the right to rest in your position as you work towards a determined destination.

On the flip side, the seat of self-discipline will give you confidence to stand when necessary. An evangelist prophesied over Yvana and me once in saying, "just as it was with David in the Bible, there will come a challenge that you will have to face in public, a challenge that you will have won multiple times and multiple ways in private. Your Goliath will come when you least expect it but you continue to prepare for that day while no one is watching. There will come a day when every eye will be on you and you cannot flinch!"

Battles will come your way, discouragement will come your way and disappointment will come your way, but if you are seated securely in self-disciplined you need not worry because you have been devoted to putting in the reps when no one knew your name.

PREPARING FOR TAKEOFF

If you cannot remain seated in self-discipline, have not committed yourself to put in the work, have not devoted yourself to preparing for destiny or have not put in the reps when no one knows you, then our wisdom is not for you. If you are ready to go for it, then this book will become your trusted friend. These practical applications of Bible, business and biomechanics will push you toward the flight of your life and give you the power to accelerate others in all that you do. We hope that you are found present for the final boarding call because the seat is yours to take. Remember, calling in itself is a signal but you have both the power and now *the push* to take action.

There will come a day when every eye will be on you and you cannot flinch!

THE BOARDING CALL

"Good afternoon passengers, this is the preboarding announcement for the flight of your life. We are now inviting those passengers with small children and any passengers requiring special assistance to begin boarding at this time. Please have your boarding pass and identification ready. Regular boarding will begin in approximately ten minutes' time. Thank you."

You are ready. Everything you need is within you. This opportunity may never come again and should you hesitate long enough, someone else will take the seat that you leave vacant despite being reserved for you. There may be challenges and moments of uncertainty but there will be plenty of growth and adventure. There are risks but you are

THE FLIGHT OF YOUR LIFE

predestined for more. You can know the joy of embracing the fullness of who you are, all that your life could mean to the world around you and all that you can become.

We encourage you to no longer live by the definitions or limitations given to you by your surroundings. Your bar is higher—much higher. This is your opportunity to make a change in focus, effort and direction that will propel you and your family faster and further than you could have possibly imagined.

If you are not the daring type, dare anyway. We dare you. We are daring you to defy gravity. This is much bigger than you yet will not be nearly as impactful without you. Contemplate all who may benefit from your daring to defy the status quo in any area or endeavor. If you are an athlete, how much more could you mean to your team if your skills improved? If you are in a committed relationship, how could your marriage or love improve if you take your seat, buckle in and make the conscious choice to be a better version of yourself? If you are a human being, see with the eyes of your soul how great of an influence you might have on the world. From the moment that you commit and take your seat, you partner with the propulsive power of potential.

Bob Marley's music won wars and helped overturn oppressive regimes around the world. Dr. King's faith and preaching became a central voice of civil rights for *all* people of color. Malcolm X's courage inspires children of all nations to live above racial injustice and mental poverty. Nelson Mandela's civil disobedience led to liberation and inspiration. These are a few of our heroes, but we ask that you fill in any person(s) you can imagine here. Their decision to take action—having heard either call or in many cases, cries of those around them—is what makes the flight of their life legendary. You may never know just how big your influence or impact might be. What matters is having taken your seat and committing to the flight of *your* life.

As Yvana and I look back, we often laugh thinking of the many challenges we have overcome. The pains, losses, literal breaks, tears and sacrifices that we have had to endure in order to live as adventurously as we do today. Those times were very hard but they were catalyst to change, catalyst to maximize our potential and propulsion. What you might desire most, your truest destiny, will not be a convenient exchange. What you feel in the core of you will not come without resistance. Potential and purpose are very unique; they will partner to push you into turbulent times, accelerate you right by what is safe or what seems logical to get you to what was always possible.

Yvana and I are being very intentional in not painting an unrealistic or overly optimistic picture of purpose or potential. There will come turbulent times where both purpose and potential are full, but your purse is not. You cannot pay rent or mortgage with purpose or potential. Sometimes, the quickest flight path to cruising altitude is the one that reminds us of how fragile we are. In other words, the higher you want to go, the lower you must become: humility. There may come a season where pursuing your purpose will mean borrowing from friends or family or your church. Committing to your purpose may mean investing savings to send yourself back to a classroom setting. There may come a turbulent moment that shakes your self-belief to the core. There may come an atmospheric shift that takes something, someone or someplace that you felt entitled to.

Charles was a world-ranked SEC champion and tore his Achilles in his first semiprofessional appearance. Yvana was an Olympic qualifier and Bahamian champion who dreamt of competing in the Olympics and was verbally committed to an Olympic berth by her national federation. A few weeks

THE FLIGHT OF YOUR LIFE

before the Olympics, we had to experience the heartbreak of finding that the federation would not honor her submission via the same newspaper that had announced her victory. Charles and I both have worked for others, exceeding their expectations and sometimes, their capabilities. Like we have, you might have been groomed for positions while being perceived as a threat who might one day take over. With elevation, there is always the probability of unexpected rough air appearing suddenly. A layoff, furlough or forced resignation without rhyme or reason can become your reality even when your performance or personality is not an issue. In your mind things are on the upswing, but when dealing with uncertainty a moment can create a turbulence that you may not have seen coming. An injury, academic setback and in 2019, a pandemic can appear without any warning and without a prompting of your own.

You may think that your big break has come, only to be surprised that these words can have a double meaning. We have been there. This is why before we proceed, it is imperative to root your next moves in your purpose even if your passion or potential presents you with problems. Your purpose must be protected and regarded as greater than passion. We urge you strongly to commit to making whatever change necessary to keeping you moving forward even if the unexpected threatens to discourage *your* progress. We encourage you to keep that edge within yourself that seeks to defy gravity and the odds against your flight. We urge you to hold fast to self-discipline and realize that there are things that are too small to pull you from that seat.

You may ask, if there is no guarantee of success in the area that I want or how I want, then what is the point of taking the risk? Let us tell you the other side of the stories we told a few moments ago. Despite the flight risks, Yvana and I remained passionately connected to propulsion and propelling others. We choose to move forward to use our momentum to mentor, inspire and to push others into greater.

Yvana did not make the Brazil Olympics but the next year, she was selected from thousands of women in a worldwide casting pool to portray the great Laila Ali in an international short film produced in Brazil that turned into an international commercial. This propelled her acting and modeling career. Yvana has been the COO of a startup that has grown in success and continues to use policies, practices and strategies that she implemented. She now serves as co-CEO of our first business, 3B Fitness and Performance. She is a global presenter and ambassador for one of the world's largest luxury motor brands and travels more than she did when she competed as a track-and-field athlete. She became a real life influence who mentors women all over the US. Companies send her promotional products and even offer her contracts and commissions based upon her reach. Her aim is to live a life worth modeling after, to be a light wherever she may be in the world.

Charles did not compete in the Olympics, but he coached his wife to her personal records and accomplishments on the track after college. Charles has earned two master's degrees and is also co-CEO of our 3B Fitness and Performance. Charles has coached professionals on the highest level of sport, some of whom have actually competed at the Olympics; he has spoken to over ten thousand students, athletes and administrators and has given messages in full auditoriums on various topics. Charles is also a working actor who has booked multiple roles in film, television and commercials. By the way, you are reading our first book produced by the experiences,

> Do not limit or allow limits on your purpose or how it may propel you.

THE FLIGHT OF YOUR LIFE

pains and struggles that are all now becoming a part of your story and propelling you forward.

Do not limit or allow limits on your purpose or how it may propel you. Enjoy the thrill of the ride and know that everything is all working out for your good. Should you accept the boarding call, you will achieve more than you could have ever imagined and others will have done the same because of you.

Good afternoon passengers, this is the final boarding announcement for the flight of your life. Your flight is ready to leave. Please make your way to the gate before the boarding doors are closed, after which no more boarding will be permitted.

Our final request as we continue: do not try to predict the way that this book will influence the propulsive impulses in you. If you find what you need, do not hesitate. Move with wisdom—but move—then come back to the book later if you need more inspiration. We challenge you to make the decision that we did—the decision to implement whatever speaks to you, moves you or becomes apparent to you as you read this book. The sky is not your limit. Time to maximize your potential.

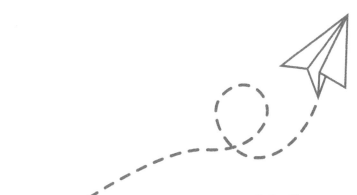

CHAPTER 2

Propulsion versus Compulsion

Whenever you feel inspired, you are being driven by something beyond yourself. It may feel like an exuberant gust of encouragement that fuels our bravery or a quiet voice within you whispering in your ear, "go for it." Think of the last time you were truly inspired. The voice you heard may have sounded like your own but had a familiarity in it, one that you have heard before. We like to call it the voice of the goal. What has been placed in you can use the tiniest of inspirations to propel you out of your lowest pit to your highest peak.

Inspiration will not leave you feeling like you are being forced against your will. Inspiration will not make you feel as if you are being dragged to your doom. If you resist being inspired, it is only because you are more focused on fear-based consequences of failure than the faith-based potential for moving forward. Somehow, we can become so inspired and simultaneously become more unsure of what is being inspired within us. We can become so focused on our fear that we forget what is inspiring about us. That is because many of us have become dependent upon motivation and have lost touch with what truly inspires us. This is a difference between propulsion and compulsion.

Motivation is something that we often attach ourselves to but inspiration attaches itself to something that is already deep within us. That is the place where imagination, creativity, hope, faith and love reside. It is the root of all the things we have the power to create that are at their best. The truth is, as we grow we also become more unfamiliar with all that is on the inside of us and we lack inspiration or reject it because we have lived in a world that runs on motivation and compulsion.

If you feel that at every waking moment you are being dragged along by the worries or fires of the day, then you are not experiencing the beauty of your design. This again is living under compulsion. If you would rather live life being pulled than pushed, then you are going to experience more of the same form of existence. You will be limiting your truest potential and truthfully, being dragged through life is nothing to become passionate about.

Propulsion is what inspires or accelerates us, while *compulsion* is what motivates and manipulates us. Living a propulsive life gives room for freedom. It allows us to live and give freely and liberally. Propulsion opens our lives to adventure and elevation. On the contrary, living under compulsion is the surrender of freedom. It obligates us, forces us or manipulates our desires and abilities that makes giving from them mandatory. It leaves us feeling empty, unfulfilled and at a loss of our true direction. Ultimately even when

> *Propulsion* is what inspires or accelerates us, while *compulsion* is what motivates and manipulates us.

we give of who we are or what we possess, living under compulsion will take what is meant to be sweet and make it bitter. We wake up and give of our talents and time but we often do so disdainfully rather than with cheer. One of our favorite verses to live by says, "each one must do just as he has purposed in his heart, not grudgingly or under compulsion, for God loves a cheerful giver."

Most of the world has learned to live under compulsion or to operate using compulsion as a tactic. It is not entirely your fault if you find yourself guilty of either. We are often raised to fear much and trust less, to take advantage or to be taken advantage of. We are judged more by what we cannot do than what we can and motivated more by consequence than the reward of either. Although the intention may be good the result leads to forfeiture of our identity, our individuality, our ability to think critically and our responsibility to use our logic and the acceptance of what *is* within our responsibility. Even as we work through the levels of formal education, we are groomed by teachers who are compelled more to meet test scores than to make a lasting impression. Even those educators whose hearts are focused on propelling the next student forward, the whole of the uniquely tailored system controls each interaction by compulsion. Yvana and I are both children of educators who have retired from the challenge of balancing their love for children and education and their compulsory requirements to educate by state mandate rather than encouraging exploration, experimentation and examination.

Living under compulsion happens when we live a purpose that does not belong to us. It is accepting the status quo or attempting to maintain it rather than to improve upon it. You may even be working in an environment where this struggle is causing you more headache and exhaustion than you can handle. That is not okay but you are. You are at

THE FLIGHT OF YOUR LIFE

a tipping point in your existence on how you want your life to be lived. We are not advocating living a life without responsibility and the flight of your life will require more attention, focus and effort than you may have given to any other thing up to this point.

Living under compulsion waiting for whatever next thing pulls you the hardest, is living under force or obligation to put out fires instead of flying high above them. Maybe you have lived so long under compulsion that you do not recognize that you have been. Other synonyms of compulsion are *convinced, coerced, persuaded, pressured, intimidated, constrained* or *controlled*. If you are being handled by external forces and pulled into things that you know are not in your best interests or the interests of those you care most about, then you are living under compulsion. Even if only temporarily, compulsory living will pull you from *the authentic self* in order to meet demands, standards or the appeasement of outside entities. Please do not misunderstand. Some entities may be external in nature yet internally linked to your internal desire or direction in which case, meeting those needs should fulfill you—like parenting or paying bills. Those are external reflections of an internal desire in manifested, tangible form.

We are taking extra care to set this point correctly as it has the power to propel your life direction and keep you moving with inspiration. As you prepare to take the flight of your life it is important that you expose yourself to inspirational people, images and environments. First, you must develop a closer relationship with self. How you speak to yourself, of yourself and concerning self can manifest or manipulate your state of mind and impact your state of movement. You will also need to consider your current relationships, not only how they influence you but how you are influencing them. As we work to elevate ourselves beyond compulsion, we may not realize a few things. First, we may have conditioned ourselves to believe that we are suffering at the hand of those around us. Second, we may not recognize that we are the compulsory force that is dragging those around us down which has impacted our state of mind and our current circumstance.

In either case, it is important to evaluate how we are giving encouraging pushes using words that accelerate others out of the dip or pit that they are in. As we inspire, we find ourselves being inspired. Whatever we sow, we reap. Whoever waters will be watered. Furthermore the more we focus on pushing others forward, the further we will find ourselves moving as we must continually create force in a positive direction that requires that we move forward and faster to propel others. As we learn to speak and move forward, we begin to hear the wind pick up and those winds whisper; even if the wind is blowing in the opposite direction than the way we desire to go, they are still saying something. The greater momentum and speed you build, the louder those whispers become. The louder they become, the easier it will be to translate the significance of those winds.

When Yvana and I first committed to each other our future and family, we created a family creed and within it contained the foundation of what we call the *propulsion test*. We vowed to assess any person or opportunity that would come to us as a couple by asking one simple question. If it did not pass the propulsion test, we would decline without blinking and move forward. Here is the propulsion test: anything or anyone who does not push us toward our destiny, propel us to maximize our potential or the potential of others we would reject. It does not matter if the opportunity appears to be or is in nature, good. If it did not meet those criteria, it was a good opportunity for someone else.

THE FLIGHT OF YOUR LIFE

One of the most significant lessons that we can give to you is knowing that not everything that appears to be good is God.

God has given you a uniquely determined destination but it is up to you to gain clarity and remain focused on that mission. It is up to you to become just as determined to focus solely on your propulsive purpose. There is nothing anyone or anything can do to keep you from it if what you desire is truly to maximize all that you are and to maximize all that will be. As we transition, we want you to keep your eyes focused forward as we unpack how propulsion can add power to your potential and pursuits.

We encourage you to begin evaluating or if necessary, eliminating individuals or items that pull you away from your authentic self. However before you do this, we also ask that you be patient as you may need to do some soul searching and genuine listening to see who that authentic self truly is. We are living in a time where those who challenge us can be written off when they are the people who we need. There are also those who may make us feel good and confident but they are actually the ones who are manipulating us, seducing us to live outside of what we are destined to do and to become. That is literally what a confidence artist or *con artist* does. If not careful these individuals can use our own insecurity, pride, arrogance or vanity against us by lulling us to sleep with compelling gestures and words, luring us or gently pulling us inch by inch out of the seat and off the path that is reserved for us.

As you continue to read, commit to filter your thoughts, decisions, conversations and actions through the propulsion test. It may be uncomfortable or seem unusual but it is useful. Your alternative is to assess each time you feel that you are being pulled away from what is important or necessary throughout the day. Take note of them. Do not react, simply take note. You will find that the root cause of living under compulsion is your submission to each pull.

RELATIONSHIPS

Relationships can be tricky, not just the romantic ones. Who we run with significantly influences our direction and can impact the speed of that direction. Evaluate whether you are in the right relationships for your goals and be sure that you too are a right relationship for theirs. Not only can we be pulled away under compulsion but we can also pull others away from their optimum potential. We can manipulate or inspire one another to take greater risks and to explore the fullness of who we could be. That is the difference between a compulsive relationship and propulsive relationships. Compulsive relationships are those with ulterior motives. Compulsive relationships are typically in relationships for what they can get and never for what they can give.

Compulsive relationships do not mind others reaching their peak as long as they have reached theirs first. They are happy when others are elevated so long as that elevation does not eclipse their own. Propulsive relationships on the other hand, view the purpose of any relationship is to help each other to reach as high as possible. Propulsive relationships understand that staying in a relationship is not nearly as important as helping the relationship along even if that means pushing the other away in order to get them to move forward. As we continue to discuss the various force implications found within these relationships, it may be a good time to take a sobering look at your relationships.

THE FLIGHT OF YOUR LIFE

> Not only can we be pulled away under compulsion but we can also pull others away from their optimum potential.

If you are wanting to lose weight and are hanging around people who have no desire or concern for their health it is likely that they are not concerned with yours as they should be. Some of our relationships are out of balance. They take or pull from us far more than they can or are willing to give. These are not always professional relationships. They often go "way back" and ultimately may be doing exactly that—keeping you back there. If your circle is not focused on forward and propelling themselves and one another it may be time to draw a new circle.

How can two people walk together if they do not agree? They will always be at odds with each other, trying to simultaneously pull each other in a direction that neither wishes to go. If your circle is not built on mutually helping one another reach the highest levels of destiny and working together to ensure both parties are connected, respected and accepted then it is not a circle; it is a line and you are in a tug of war. You are both anchored to one another and are neither going forward or backwards but most certainly not upward. These relationships are solely based upon how one can benefit most and gain advantage over the other.

These relationships are sometimes the most stifling form of compulsive relationships as they are undetected and misidentified. These relationships are known as *terminal* relationships. If you have ever flown commercial you have likely spent time in a holding location waiting for your flight or upon arrival. Like airport terminals these relationships are often wonderful stops along our journey but they do not serve a long-term purpose other than to be there when needed. They are better served as transient encounters. Terminals give comfort between flights or during periods of transition when no flight is occurring. Some relationships that we desperately want to compel to be more are only intended to be terminal. These relationships may refresh and refuel us in between departures but any prolonged encounters expose our need to depart before either of us feels obligated to share space.

This is why Yvana and I assess each relationship we enter and allow into our lives with propulsive intent. We seek early whether there is a mutual desire to propel each other into our greatest impact. This is what it means to be in a *right relationship*. Right relationship is propulsive and may be gauged by the exhibiting of the appreciation of differences in opinion, boldness to stand for right, humility to accept and admit when wrong, a conscious willingness to push beyond limitations and challenging each other to live above the status quo.

Right relationships are never forced. They fit. Not every relationship is that simple but generally, there is an internal connection to something on the inside of another that ignites a desire to see great things for them; you sense that there is a mutual desire to see your life shine just as brightly. It has been our experience that when a relationship feels forced, projects neediness, clinginess, requires far too much attention, is inauthentic, is untrustworthy or shows no forward trajectory it is not worth pursuing. Period. Allow us to reiterate, we make every effort to avoid basing our relationships on what others can do for us. We intentionally begin many of our relationships with offering whatever we can to propel others forward first without looking for return. Our strongest bonds have often come from propelling others into new levels of thinking or living. As the popular quote says, "hang out with us long enough and we will brainwash you into believing in yourself and that you can do anything."

When we are approached and presented with the possibility of being in a relationship with someone we also try to understand what inspired them. Is it our personality, faith, accomplishments, ambition or the strength of our marriage? We use this tool on ourselves also as it helps to keep us from trying to compel others to be in relationship with us! It is a means of protecting not only our best interests but of those we encounter.

When anyone says that they want to be in a friendship relationship we take the word *friend* very seriously. To be called a friend of ours is the ultimate level of trust for us. It requires more than sharing a few good times. Being in a relationship means being available in times of drought or adversity not just being there when things feel nice or convenient. It means sincerity in identity, being comfortable with having biases challenged. It means enjoying dealing with hard truths and being dedicated to helping us deal with hard truths of our own. These are how we gauge propulsive relationships that can become great personal friendships. A word to the wise: compulsive relationships will expose themselves pretty quickly if you pay attention.

Business and professional relationships are not so easy to navigate. You may have heard the saying, "never mix friendship and business." That does not mean that we should be jerks or unfriendly while doing business. It also does not mean avoid having friends in business, as you may interpret. The phrase points back to keeping right relationships with healthy professional boundaries and expectations. It means focusing on propulsive purpose organizationally, moving the mission and message forward before that of the friendship.

PROPULSION VERSUS COMPULSION

It is found in keeping clarity of mind and mission above that of the relationship. It is embracing a means of protecting the organization from operating under compulsion. Compulsion can kill commerce and corporation. Compulsion in business relationships leads to cutting corners, undermining or undervaluing the client and customer and sweeping ethics out of the boardroom.

While pursuing an EMBA, I became very interested in the impact of compulsion on business relationships. I found that compulsion is a vortex that pulls decision makers and would-be leaders into *group think*. Group think is an avoidable and potentially dangerous rut where individuals go along with a direction that is counterproductive or inefficient to the progress of the mission and vision of a company. It stems from not fostering a community of right relationships. This impacts honesty, truthfulness and objectiveness in an effort to not offend or disrupt the cultural status quo. It is rooted in fear and is typically a sign of an organization that is too authoritarian, top-down or on the brink of a meltdown from within. They typically appear friendly on the surface but under the cover is a weak leadership structure that thrives on submission and subjugation.

You may work in an environment like this. Do not immediately turn in your resignation after reading this! Besides if you are dedicated to challenge the structure and the status quo for the betterment of the entire organization, there will come a time when you may be asked to resign—not because of your performance but because of what your presence means to the mobilization of others who would do the same. On the other hand, you may be at a point where it is better to resign than to remain in an environment that does not want to grow or is not ready to do so. That is the mark of someone determined to remain in right relationships. It may also be *the goal* within you propelling you to take flight like a mother eagle who puts briers and brambles in the nest to push her young to take the flight of their life.

If you are feeling that you are facing this situation do not be alarmed. Your departure is not an indication that there is something wrong with you. You may very well be an excellent team player and you may be misinterpreted as being full of selfish ambition. Do not allow any form of compulsion to pull you back if *the goal* is pushing you forward. Most importantly above all other relationships, the most important relationship to remain in right relationship with is the one you have with yourself. If you need to make calculated moves in order to maximize propulsion toward your determined destination, then trust that unction and move forward. Leaving to pursue something better is a sign of maturity and clarity of focus. It does not always suggest something is wrong. Just be sure that you have done what you need to do to give yourself the best chance at keeping the momentum to move forward. It is more professional and propulsive to make your move for better than to move out of bitterness. It is called *pivot strategy*. You are still moving, you are still producing force. You are still propelling and being propelled. Accept that you may have grown bigger than your current environment, and focus on going as fast and as far as you were designed to.

RESPONSIBILITIES

Another day, another list. Tasks to order. Put on your work self. Show up early, expect to leave late. Affirmations. Positive self-talk. Interruption. Finish that later. Later. I'm late (hope no one noticed). Pretend to like Brad. "Hi, Brad." Jump right into work. Profit, profit, profit. Presentation. Stay in your lane. Wait, they need me out of my lane now. How am I being scolded for...? They literally asked me to take care of that. Now I am behind on my deadline. New project. Wait, I have to finish...Jericha came up with the idea so why was I asked to do her work? Got it done. Finished. Here, Jericha. Jericha makes one edit, takes all the credit. It's 6:45 already? My daughter's game. Oh no, it started at six. Pretend you saw the entire game. We need groceries. Order takeout. Brush teeth. Shower? Bed. Alarm. Another day...

You may identify with this scenario but before you get anxiety from reliving the cycle in your mind, breathe and realize that was only an illustration. We have been there. Do not beat yourself up. You are surviving. We want you to thrive as much as we are certain that you would like to. There is massive potential in your current circumstance and within your current position and responsibilities. If you are willing to shift your perspective a little you will be able to reverse-engineer compulsive obligations and convert them into propulsive power that can help you on the flight of your life. The power of propulsion may be applied to these mechanisms.

The wind and weight of these responsibilities may come spinning violently but they can be harnessed and used to increase your efficiency and capability. There will always be assigned responsibilities thrown at you or dropped in your lap. You have one of two choices: buckle under the pressure or buckle up for the ride. Every pressure that you face is bottled for your propulsion. Run toward the pressure. The power that could be released in your life could send your entire family to the highest level of the stratosphere if you are observant enough on where to focus it.

The example that we used above is one of many to illustrate how responsibilities can get out of whack if we let them. The issue is how we manage them and how we utilize tools to keep what is important, important. Yes some things require sacrifice. But you can decide what gets to be sacrificed and that should be anything that impedes your purpose. Note that we did not say your profit. One of our friends says it this

THE FLIGHT OF YOUR LIFE

way. "Learn to keep the main thing, the *main* thing." It will take a little work to prioritize what is actually important and to discern what we feel compelled to manage that are neither ours nor are as urgent as we may have convinced ourselves of being.

How often do you start the day with one or two things that you really want to get done or experience but then you look back on the day and you have done everything else except those things? This is what we mean. Responsibilities also need boundaries and so do we. We need to be honest and upfront with our commitments and avoid committing to things that we could do rather than what we know we *must* do. As Yvana and I coach athletes and business professionals we often help them assess exactly how much time they are spending on things that have no bearing on their productivity or progress. For some it requires setting up timers, turning off notifications or restricting access to apps. We also recommend setting access limits for them. Not every text needs an immediate response. Not every phone call requires an immediate callback. What does, *does*. But typically you know the difference.

> Every pressure that you face is bottled for your propulsion. Run toward the pressure.

Some things we need to complete because they are tied to our purpose. They may not be convenient and they may not even be comfortable but they are a part of keeping the main thing the main thing. Some things feel compulsive because we have procrastinated to the point where pressure has mounted. Suck it up and get it done. That is all that we will say about that. Regarding the tasks that are a part of our role or function there are mindsets that can help make these responsibilities a little less burdensome.

The first step is to define your big long-term goals. We are not suggesting that you have some random goals in your head but clearly defined goals that will serve as the umbrella that will cover whatever it will take to achieve that outcome. Then you must identify one key area that this outcome falls under. We suggest limiting it to four key areas that pertain to life: personal, which could be spiritual, social, familial or intellectual; financial, which could include career, income, savings, investing, or giving; relationship, which could include marriage, dating, professional relationships, mentors, network, etc.; health or performance, which could include weight loss, nutrition, sports, physique or marathon, etc. Remember, you only get four key areas.

After you establish these goals, you need to write down why each of these things matters so much to you in one to two sentences for each desired outcome. It needs to be simple and easy to understand. This will make it easy to comprehend why you are doing what you are doing. It will also clarify why you are excited or inspired to do whatever is required. We will discuss this more in a minute. This is more than simply defining your *why*. Many people have heard of this but it is more important to comprehend your why than to be compelled by the idea of your *why*.

Now we can establish the how. If you are going to see a particular result in your life in one of these areas you must make a clear plan. The plan should not be an entire blueprint but three to four things that you must do to establish or to achieve what you desire. You will hear rather quickly a few things that will come to mind. It may be to sell your car. It may be going to school. It may be to get some help. It may be to hire someone. Whatever comes to mind write it down before your inspiration is hijacked by fear of failure or compulsion.

There are two more steps. Next, define two or three milestones that will help make your desired outcome most likely to become reality. An example might be someone who wants to write a book. A milestone may be to get a publisher or to

THE FLIGHT OF YOUR LIFE

self-publish. Another milestone might be to get a website for their book. Another milestone might be to sell their first one thousand copies. Each of these milestones will need smaller tasks in order for them to be complete. Define ten or less tasks for each milestone that must be done in order to complete the desired goal and come up with a reward that you will treat yourself to once a milestone has been achieved.

After doing this, repeat the process for the three other key areas of purpose and give each overarching objective an individual deadline. You have to give it a deadline. They may be adjusted but *give yourself a deadline*. Then establish answers to these milestones with the following: who else will this benefit if I accomplish this goal besides myself? *Who else will this inspire or propel forward? How will this goal create opportunities for others?*

What you have done is create a pipeline to purpose, a *flight plan*. When you look at what you have written you will see what you are really after. You will also establish that everything in your life has a place and particular purpose in propelling you toward these outcomes. When things come up, you can look back to your flight plan and see if and where these proposed or imposed responsibilities line up with your outcomes. Every day you can set aside a few minutes to read your flight plan. Here is a tip. Make that a part of your morning routine, whip out your sheets, say a prayer, then write three observations before you begin your day in a journal by your bed or at your coffee table. You will want to write three things: one thing I am grateful for, one thing I look forward to today and one assertive statement I will repeat to myself throughout the day.

Let's make this a little more applicable to the example that we opened with but with these new tools in mind.

PROPULSION VERSUS COMPULSION

Morning, wake up. New habit. Start the day with gratitude. I am grateful for, looking forward to, and will be assertive.

My personal goal is to become a director in three years or less and that starts with today. I am going to show up early because it is what *I want to do not because anyone expects me to*. My daughter has a soccer game and one of my goals is to have a healthier work-life balance. *I am going to create a hard stop* on work when my daughter has a game at 5:45 PM no exceptions.

Where work stops will be here tomorrow. Jericha and I can prep before the meeting. She has a family too and *I choose to respect* her work-life balance by establishing mine. One of my goals is to build healthier relationships with my coworkers. Brad, how are you? Sincerely, I apologize that I never really ask you how things are going. *I will do better* at that. Is there anything I can do to help you today? If there is, my only ask is that you give me a heads-up before popping in and give me as much time as I need to really give you and the job the attention you deserve.

I want to build my professional network which will ultimately help my sales numbers because *I am genuinely interested in building relationships*. Regarding the project how else can I show my skills and *position myself for advancement* if I am not offered the work? Since I was offered the work, I *choose to lead* the project and use it to form a better relationship with Jericha by meeting with her *instead of assuming* that I have to complete the entire project myself.

This is a great opportunity to grow my skills and *I actually need to learn* how to navigate relationships with my peers and *encourage their skills as a resource* and also *get first-hand experience* with what it really takes to build this thing. If I am aiming to be a director then *I can take this opportunity* to establish standard operating procedures that will come in handy when I have to lead a project like this in the future. And if *I establish my team correctly* I have a couple of people that I would always want to work with and *that I can trust* to delegate.

    I want to make sure that things like this are easy to replicate so they can improve and *I can be a supportive leader* who *sets my direct reports up for success*. Leaving work *on my time* gave me enough buffer to be on time for the game. Today, *I chose to be intentional* regarding my relationships and goals and *this is only the beginning*. My daughter's game is over. A quick stop at the supermarket and her favorite post-game delivery is on its way. *I am a super mom*. Today, I felt in control. Even when things happened outside of my control, I could see how they were adding movement to my desired outcomes. And now since I left work at work, I am going to take a little time with my boo, watch one mindless thing, set my social media app timer for thirty minutes, and then I am going to bed.

    You can put your own goals and experiences in this story. It is not hard to see how defining your desired outcomes can have a dramatic impact on keeping your eyes focused forward and your progress pushing toward your clearly defined goals. As a standard practice we ask our clients to finish their day with five minutes of reflection and jotting that down in a journal. Identify three things in particular:

1. What made me happy today?

2. What was one lesson I learned today?

3. What was a big deal, big win or big achievement today?

    Do this for enough days, and these days begin to take on new meaning.

PROPULSION VERSUS COMPULSION

At this particular point in your journey these tools will help you internally reconcile whatever compulsions you may be sensing, every project or distraction and reverse the polarity. Take what was once negative and see how and where it can be used to bring about your long-term desired outcomes. Doing this will inject your passion into the core of whatever comes your way. As you continue to journal each day, you will begin to see the patterns developing that are directing you toward your goals. Once a responsibility or obligation has been given to you, *you own it*.

That means that it belongs to you. You can make it work for yourself and as a means of working toward your desired outcomes. Set your bar as high as you can. Go after it not to impress your employer but to impress yourself. Do what has never been done before. Come at it from a new angle. Be innovative and creative. Shine brightly and do not do it for vain recognition. You are recognizing your true capability and it will serve you well. If someone tries to compel you to dim your light do not do it. Lisa Nichols says, "if they cannot stand your light, make them put on shades." Yvana always adds, "better yet, give them your shades and walk away."

The book *How to Become CEO* written by Jeffrey Fox encourages us to "leave people with the weight of who we are." Some people will gravitate and some will repel. That is not up to you. We either live under the weight of others—spiritually, emotionally, professionally—or we push against that which does not belong to us. That requires self-discipline and a clear definition of where we are trying to go and where we hope to propel others. This will keep you mindful that you are willfully choosing your flight path. You have been chosen and predestined for good works so choose to partner with that.

When you partner with propulsion—pushing the envelope of your gifts, skills, talents and abilities—you are establishing greater purpose. Having this type of clarity will push your name into rooms and conversations that you have yet to be personally invited into. With the level of self-discipline you manage your responsibilities, you will either find a seat at the table or eventually establish a seat on your own. Habitually choose propulsion over compulsion and watch as you begin to carve a niche for yourself.

These tools are tai chi for your soul. You must be patient and work on this tool consistently. Continue to tool yourself with skills that will put you in a propulsive position. Use each day to build using the responsibilities that come your way. A proper runway for your takeoff is being prepared. You just keep focusing on the key aspects of *your* being and you will see an amazing turnaround in the way you see your responsibilities.

REHEARSALS

The mind and its connection to our body is extremely fascinating. What we truly think is what we are, there's no way around it. Who we are is a sum of what we repeatedly do. We are hardwired to make our most frequent impulses our reality. There is a unique system called the *motor cortex* within your brain. It is where your true potential lies. This area of the brain is where our nerve impulses originate and initiate muscular *action*. As we have already discussed the more these thoughts occur, the greater the signal of the potential becomes. The greater the magnitude of these signals, the greater the impulse to move upon that potential. This is an oversimplified approach to how we all take action every day but it also gives us insight into how we may begin voluntarily choosing propulsion and refusing to live under compulsion. This requires *self-control*.

PROPULSION VERSUS COMPULSION

If you are going to live a life that is propulsive you must consciously choose to propel forward. If at any moment, you feel that you are not actively engaged in exercising your choice to move life forward, take back your control and choose your destiny over your discouragement or disadvantage. Take back your ability to act. Take back your ability to respond. Take back your response-ability. You have the power of propulsion and can tell your potential what it will do. If you are not where you want to be you must choose to direct all of your potential in the direction of your greatest life experience. The flight of your life is the journey made by choice. The flight of your life is the ability to choose your propulsion over powerlessness. No matter what you may encounter the more you decide at this moment from this moment on to live on purpose, you will always maximize your potential and encourage others to do the same.

Psychologist Dr. Srini Pillay suggests that our minds can be reprogrammed for successful living. In an online interview he expressed, "our brains are wired so that we go on the same patterns over and over again even when we think we are doing something differently. The reason that we continue to fail in life or refuse to take action is that we would rather master disappointment and self-sabotage than to seek our own fulfilment." He adds, "we do not realize that the action of not taking action is a means of intentionally keeping our own selves stuck in a predictable pattern. We naturally want to become very good at the fact that our life sucks."

In sport science we refer to this as the chronic or permanent adaptations of *rehearsal*. Rehearsal is a means of coding into the mental and physical systems of our actions to create patterns that become second nature or most readily accessible when a change or disturbance is encountered. That is in its purest form, what we are illustrating as we discuss potential and power, propulsion and compulsion. In the same fashion as athletes become more proficient and efficient at repeatable tasks, your brain is programmed to do the same thing in every area of your life. You may actually be more efficient at rehearsing patterns than a world-class athlete and never even knew it. You may have ascribed to the compulsory notion that you are a product of your environment when in fact you are living in a product of *your* environment. You have always had the power to rehearse your most dominant signals. Even when you have chosen to take no action inactivity has become your default. You may be fully maximizing your potential to do nothing or nothing more than what you are doing today. Let that sink in for a moment.

> The flight of your life is the ability to choose your propulsion over powerlessness.

Allowing our environment to be the deciding factor of who we are and will become is living under compulsion. Compulsory rehearsal limits our lifestyle, personality and pursuits to replication, reproduction or regurgitation. You do not have to repeat any cycle that you do not wish to continue—that is for certain. You can propel yourself further and further away from your default settings by rehearsing what it is you would like to see changed within your life.

Yvana and I are both former world-class athletes and we have had the privilege of coaching other world-class athletes and corporate athletes who are MVPs at home. Before we begin working with any individual we begin with assessments that expose areas of movement inefficiency, limitation, restriction or risk. We intentionally expose our clients to a battery of tests that expose their defaults. We then present our findings to each client to help them see how they have trained their body to move naturally and the issues those patterns cause in their performance. Just because there are things that you have *always* done and a version of yourself you have *always* been does not mean that it is the way that you must remain.

Too often we submit our authority to that of habit. You may have always acted in a particular way but that is not who you are. That is what you are rehearsing to be. You may have always reacted in a particular way but that is not who you are. That is what you are rehearsing to be. You may have always quit when things become challenging but that is not who you are. That is what you are rehearsing to be. You may fill in any particular default thinking, speech or action. Ultimately, you will come to the conclusion as we have: you are a reproduction of what you rehearse. You are a skilled actor who has rehearsed so well that you have convinced yourself that it is your only and ultimate reality. If you want to change your reality, change your rehearsal.

One of the most powerful tools that you have at your disposal is words. Words have more potential within them than all of the nuclear plants in existence. We have the inherent power to impact everything we see and know through our words and limiting the words we receive that are not ours. We may not be aware of just how many words we are speaking or receiving throughout each day, yet we do not look around and see how our words are the world we are living in.

You may recall that we encounter over ten thousand marketing messages each day but that is a drop in a bucket when compared to the messages that we voluntarily expose ourselves to digitally. Think about how many words you hear in a day in every digital form you can imagine: computer, phone, Facebook, Instagram, Tiktok, YouTube, news reports, e-mail, text, television shows, movies, podcasts or music. We engage in all or versions of these digitally distributed words multiple times throughout the day. Our entire world is shaped by words. We have not mentioned the words that

THE FLIGHT OF YOUR LIFE

we say to ourselves or to others internally or aloud during the course of the day. Words that are withheld are still heard deep within our minds and our motor cortex; it takes all of these in and moves us into action to make them a reality even if it means no movement at all.

Words have potential and propulsive power, which is why we stress to you that maximizing your potential is necessary but where that potential is being directed is crucial. *The power of life and death are in the tongue*. That scripture should make our point crystal clear. Whether you truly live a propulsive life or exist in a perpetual life-sucking vortex until the moment of your passing is all predicated by your words. Stephen Hawking could no longer speak and yet his words are still impacting thought today.

Everything in life is voice activated. The technology that was used to communicate Mr. Hawking's thoughts were triggered by his neural impulses then translated into existence. That technology is amazing, however it is not new. It is an electronic replication of how our lives actually work:

If you want to change your reality, change your rehearsal.

Watch your thoughts, they become your words; watch your words, they become your actions; watch your actions, they become your habits; watch your habits, they become your character; watch your character, it becomes your destiny.

PROPULSION VERSUS COMPULSION

Our suggestion to you is to actively engage in choosing when to *say more* or *say less*, when to listen *more* or to listen *less*. This simplifies your rehearsal to something that you can grasp without feeling overwhelmed. When faced with an observed lack or need do not simply state the facts of which you are already aware. It is much *less* about the facts of your current status and *more* about the potential of impacting that reality. Choose to invest your words into how you might change your current situation and the time available or necessary for you to do so. When you observe your day being consumed by fear, worry or anxiety, do not continue to allow sources that are feeding the impulses to more anxiety to have access to your motor cortex. It is *more* about taking control of your emotional well-being and much *less* about who or where the source of information is coming. When faced with a default reaction or response, do not lean into compulsion. Compose yourself then proceed with propulsive words and actions that reflect your destiny in that moment. Obviously, that may mean doing what is necessary to protect yourself or others. Self-control does not necessarily mean avoiding conflict or choosing to ignore the call to stand for what is right.

Accept that you are not a product of your environment. Accept that you do not have to repeat what you have rehearsed. Accept that you have response-ability. Accept that you have the potential and the power to choose what you rehearse. The old saying "practice makes perfect" is incorrect. The alternative, "practice makes permanent," is also incorrect. We submit to you that "practice makes *programmed*." What you rehearse is never permanent, it is programmed. Therefore it is programmable. You can program propulsion as the default setting of your actions and reactions but it will require rehearsal. So start practicing what you preach and watch how your reality begins to change daily.

THE FLIGHT OF YOUR LIFE

RUMBLINGS

Upon takeoff you may perceive the rumblings of wind as you push forward. They can be disturbing but they are great indicators that you are maximizing your power and propelling faster. This rumbling is an early indication of peer dissatisfaction with your persistent progress or at the early signs of change. Rumblings are those little whispers, words in passing, rumors or undertones intended to keep you in place to check you. They may come in the form of insult, intimidation, rumors or pushback intended to compel you to stop making progress or to quit pushing forward. You may have grown to ignore many of them over time but there is a subtle opportunity to maximize potential that you may have yet to recognize was unique to only you.

As a young girl Yvana would often be teased for her height, personality, uniquely deep sultry voice and other physical attributes that she developed *early*. Changes like these led her to question why she was made the way she had been. She questioned her voice being so sultry as a teenager. Adults would often comment on the maturity in her sound and make jokes that would leave her scarred. She questioned why she was taller and more fit than many of her classmates. She wanted to believe that she was beautiful and would look at herself in the mirror, studying the features that she would be teased for. Yvana would even be disciplined by her grandmother for spending time in the mirror, (Anyone who has an old-school granny knows that any time in the mirror was vanity.). The truth was Yvana like many young girls, was standing face-to-face with her own insecurities when she looked in the mirror.

Those rumblings were all indicators of where she was heading. There is no resistance for objects at rest. There is no force acting upon them. If you are experiencing the

PROPULSION VERSUS COMPULSION

rumblings of rumor, bullying, constant jokes or reprimand, you would be missing the point if you focus on them and not what they mean. It makes us sad to hear of young people who harm themselves or others because they do not yet comprehend this. You too may still have wounds from younger years or are experiencing these rumblings as you work to make a career or name for yourself in your current role.

You may also have lived long enough to recognize that some things in your past have actually made you stronger or had given you greater determination toward your destiny. "Hindsight is twenty-twenty." That is the truth of looking back or actively listening to the rumblings around you today. Everything in life is not face value. There may be words said concerning you in passing, things that you feel ostracized, teased or mocked for. Do not be compelled to believe these words as indication that something is wrong with you but that there may be something right with you. There may be something that is right with you that you are approaching in the wrong way but that only means that you must listen even more intently to the rumblings of the wind.

The truth is humans have a bent toward attaching our emotional distress to others or dumping our fears or incapability upon others. We want to make ourselves feel good and we want to feel like we are not losing. In order to feel like a winner we can attempt to make others feel like losers so that they will not have the advantage or a clear distinction beyond the level that we perceive ourselves. You see it all the time and may even be doing the same thing, forgiving your intentions and judging everyone else by their actions. Life is full of posers. There are those who present themselves to be rich but are literally broke, those who focus solely on their appearances despite

> There is no resistance for objects at rest. There is no force acting upon them.

feeling unattractive and undesirable. Those who downplay the exceptional talents or gifts of others in a pompous attempt to show expertise when they themselves struggle with feelings of inadequacy and fraud.

These rumblings are not always as they seem. Given Newton's law concerning equal but opposite actions as you perceive the rumblings of compulsory and coercive pushback against your progress and propulsion, then you are on the right track. This is a necessary pressure and pressure is a privilege. Every day that you hear the rumblings you should know that you are creating momentous change in your environment and in the people around you. You may not be around to see just how far the impact of your presence goes or the impact of the speed of your propulsion but know that it is creating momentum that will accelerate your family, your team, your peers in ways that they may never be able to credit you enough for.

Yvana was made fun of for things like her voice, her shoe size and her stature. She kept moving forward and chief among her accomplishments in life, she met Charles Larry Bailey Jr. from Biloxi, Mississippi. Nothing else matters much after that but for your sake, I will continue her story. Those same qualities that she had been teased for would later prove to be the very things that were custom fit for her. They had been intentionally designed to propel the flight of her life. Those same size-11 shoes and long legs would lead her to compete for and win multiple state championships. They would later afford her a full track scholarship and an opportunity to walk away from her university with a bachelor's and master's degree with zero student-loan debt. Those same legs would prove to be native to her ancestry and would eventually propel her to compete and win her first Bahamas National Championship and meet Olympic qualification standards.

PROPULSION VERSUS COMPULSION

That very deep and sultry voice would later propel her into opportunities to perform as a lead vocalist on a ministry platform that literally reaches tens of thousands on any given weekend even during a pandemic. Her voice has helped her to sing backup vocals on professional recordings, has booked her in spokesman and voice work. It has breathed life into characters on screen and off-Broadway productions. That same personality would provide her roles in television seen around the world in international, national and regional spots. She has emceed for conferences and serves as a professional brand spokesperson for one of the premiere luxury car brand manufacturers in the world.

Those same muscles and hands were featured internationally for another car brand as she portrayed one of the greatest boxers of all time, Laila Ali. The time in the mirror has led her to book live modeling jobs on television and some runways. In her thirties, Yvana is consistently booked as a fitness model, health and fitness ambassador for multiple brands and is a brand media influencer. She is a professional trainer and co-CEO of our performance training business. She mentors women of all ages and is a life and relationship coach to many out of the wisdom and love that God has put in her heart to see other people move forward. This is not a comprehensive list of all that she is or does. The woman is genuinely a unicorn.

The purpose of her story is to inspire you to hear the whispers in the winds of rumblings around you. Bring anything up to the level you need it to be that is meant to discourage, destroy your confidence or to quiet your voice. Whatever and whoever compels you to forfeit your uniqueness, gifts or abilities should be listened to not for what they are saying at face value but what their words or disapproval means in regard to approval of yourself.

THE FLIGHT OF YOUR LIFE

The next individual who calls you stupid is whispering to you in rumbles of wind: "you are brilliant and your unique ability to do the impossible intimidates and exposes me." The next time someone says that you will never amount to anything, hear the whisper in the rumble: "you are worth more than you realize and I fear that you may realize and propel right from under my control and comfort." The next time you are told that you are not good enough hear the whisper in the rumbling wind say: "all that you are is far better and more than *enough*. I am not good enough for you."

Rumblings like these are only capable of speaking to your present not your propulsion. You may neither be currently capable or prepared for whatever your end goal may be but that is the beauty of *taking* the flight of *your* life. If their words hurt and cut deep, cry if you have to but decide to interpret what those tears mean.

ROUSINGS

Rousing is a very interesting word. It reflects whatever gives expression and breathes life into inanimate places or excites us. For instance, what you have been reading thus far is intended to stir up the gifts within you. It is our hope that we spur you on to do and create better. If you feel that our words and stories exhilarate and electrify your feeling that anything is possible, then we are hitting the appropriate buttons that should ignite the fire within you that have the combustible power to move you forward. However as passionate as we are about seeing you do that, we cannot give our passion to you. We can only hope that you discover at your core what lights you up more than anything in the world then giving you the courage to run toward it.

We want to invigorate that part of you with extra care to not move you through motivational speech alone but to inspire you to dig deeper into your soul, mind and emotions. This is the type of rousing that you can feel in your skin like fire trapped inside of your cells. Much like how our world is designed the greatest pressure is internal and has the power to propel you faster than you thought possible once released. When our brain signals our motor units to fire we do not perceive the signal, but we become aware of movement. Likewise you may not necessarily *feel* that you are being propelled, but it will not be long that you will become aware of what *moves* you.

What truly *moves* you, propels you? You do not need any pumping or priming. You do not need to be dragged for what *moves* you. This is another difference between motivation and inspiration. Motivation is not connected to our eternal self. It is living at the surface. A nice car does not *move* you, but it may motivate you. A diverse portfolio does not *move* you but it can motivate you. A position or a title does not *move* you but it can motivate you. What moves you is what gives any meaning to what motivates. What moves you is inspiration. Whenever you see it, you feel it and it feels you. This is far more than emotion, it is something supernatural. It is naked, pure and vulnerable. That is the goal—to live with that unidentifiable *knowing* that you are on the *right path*.

What moves you is attached to the legacy within you. It is tied to forever. It is powered by eternity. Every time you encounter it, it moves you to tears. You cannot explain it but you know that you do not need to. In that moment you no longer feel, you *know*. In that moment there is clarity of purpose, potential and propulsion. It is as if all of the heavenly bodies stand in alignment around you and you see yourself for the first time. No matter what you are currently doing or may be currently after at that moment, you would give it all up just to have that moment become yours. That is your moment. You must partner with that and put yourself in a propulsive position and allow *the goal* to propel you through whatever may come in order to live that moment for life.

Speaking of *that* moment you may have already chosen to do whatever it takes to meet it. You may have even crafted the flight plan and have actively been engaging in the steps to get there. Yet there will come certain moments that do not feel so good. You must remain confident enough to continue pushing toward the moments that you want most. Not every moment along the way will mean as much to us but they can actually mean so much more to others who watch how we handle them.

Your job is to trust that all things are working together for good. There are conditions, but *anyone who seeks, finds*. To *anyone who knocks the door will be opened*. You have already chosen to invest your full self into maximizing your potential. You must give it time to see exactly what and who it is that you are moving to. You may be surprised to find out just how much larger than you this thing you are moving really is. You may have only received a glimpse of all that you were meant to accomplish. Even when you do not feel like you are moving just know that you are. Keep moving forward. If it requires big faith then know that it is most likely a big mountain or big masses.

> There are conditions, but *anyone who seeks, finds*. To *anyone who knocks the door will be opened*.

Never make light of what truly moves you and also pay attention to your pain. Your pain may be your greatest preparation. Your hurt can make room for healing. Your struggles can construct the framework on which you build your success. The things that move us to tears confirm our course and communicate our character and clues to our career. It is what makes you identify with romantic comedy. Your

PROPULSION VERSUS COMPULSION

desire to see others find love and to find it in their happily ever after could be a legitimate vehicle of purpose. Maybe you identify with the underdog who overcomes their adversity or adversary. Your desire to see others grow to believe in themselves and become champions in life or an arena is a legitimate vehicle of purpose. Maybe you weep every time you hear of a young mother losing a child to drugs or violence. Your desire to bring counsel and healing or justice and reform is a legitimate vehicle of purpose. Maybe you cry for joy as unknown athletes bite their Olympic medals and maybe you weep bitterly when you see the marginalized, elderly, oppressed or the helpless treated as anything less than human.

That feeling on the inside of you that feels right—the whisper behind you saying, "this is the way. Walk in it" —can be trusted. The words are propelling you forward and come with a promise to never leave or to abandon you. There may be times when you are walking by yourself but we can attest that you are never actually alone. In order to chart new territory and to go where you have never been before, that is the adventure. If any of these applications and scenarios resonate within you then you may have just been reunited with *your* purpose. That is only the beginning. This is where many conclude their journey prematurely.

Did you have a moment as you read through those examples? If you did were you immediately met with uninvited guests, words and thoughts that pulled you back to reality? Did you immediately shrug off the feeling as if what you connected to was not real? You do not have to accept that. The rousing that was happening was quickening your spirit. You may not have connected with our examples but maybe you felt something. Instead of dismissing what you felt see if it lines up with the flight plan you have written for yourself and if you haven't yet we encourage you to go back and do it. You can make that feeling real and make that moment materialize. That is the reality of faith. The facts will catch up and fall in line but do not dismiss those moments.

Before it can slip away again write down what you are feeling at this moment. Write about any situation that truly *moves* you. Ask yourself, "why does this move me?" then write your response. Once you have successfully written down these three things ask yourself this one question in two parts: "what is the problem that I see in the scenario and how would I solve it?" Surprisingly your responses may rouse you and propel you to action. It may also give you the insight that you need to begin the work of removing the limiters in your life by giving you a target to make progress toward.

Maybe your answers reflect an immediate action you can take to create change in an area you are truly moved by. A business idea could present itself in the form of a product or service that would meet the need of hundreds or thousands of people who are in need for it. Your answers may not necessarily be all that entrepreneurial. Each answer may give you your next steps. Maybe it is more education or asking your employer to include you in meetings on the subject. You may be moved to research companies that are already offering solution-based services like those you imagine. There may be an opportunity to get involved. However as you answer these questions, realize that they mean most to you because they are tied to your legacy but they will not happen without you.

As a final word of propulsion it is time to make moves. This is the flight of your life. Every moment is a new adventure. You are ready to propel yourself and others and there is nothing that can stop you. Do not fear failure. We do not fail because we cannot do great things. We fail because we do not do great things with our life. Whatever excuses you may have rehearsed up to this moment—like not having enough time, support or education—is no longer valid. There are people who have the same level of education and training as you do and the same upbringing, struggles and disadvantages as you have. Yet they propelled themselves every day from the pit to what is possible while you sit each day on your full potential barely scratching the surface. Enough!

This is the day that you get up and pick up whatever it is that you know has been given to you by God. Finish the good work that was started *in* you. Whatever it takes whatever it is whoever it requires, you must get there! Other people are waiting for you to get there. Their life depends on it. No limits and no limiters allowed. It is time to do the real work. Having the limiters in our lives removed is not always easy but if you are intending to take flight toward these goals, you must be sure that you can reach the appropriate speeds before takeoff. Otherwise you will barrel down the runway and have to abort the takeoff before you take flight.

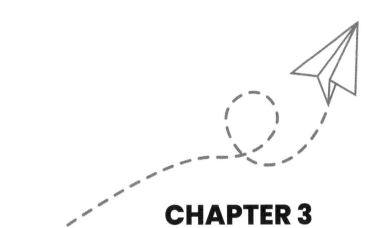

CHAPTER 3

Power and Potential

You have incredible potential. We are confidently assuming that you are aware of this or have heard it said to you before. The question has always been how does one fully access the power of their potential? How do you make your *potential* your superpower? So many have great potential but no matter how hard they try, they can never seem to get their world to reflect that greatness. It is because most of us do not truly understand what potential is. So allow us to try to simplify the topic a bit.

Potential and power meet at the intersection of *potentiation*. We know it's a fancy word but there is so much to gather from this one word. Potentiation is the prepotential. It is the action before the action that we recognize. It is the unseen and unperceived happenings between our mind and body. So when people say that you have great potential what they are truly saying is there is a great connection between your mind and your ability to create positive momentum or actions in the direction of your goals. They could also be recognizing that there is a great deal of opportunity for you to do much good but there is a disconnect between your brain and body. What your mind is trying to push you to do your body is being pulled away by distractions that are keeping you from maximizing the potential that you have been given.

You may have heard the saying "whatever you feed the most gets stronger." That is in essence how potentiation works. Whatever you give your energy or whatever impulses you allow to have the greatest influence in your life get stronger and more influential. That is the only caveat. Potential does not recognize positive or negative actions it only cares about action.

You may have a difficult time with this but you are currently living out the potential that you have chosen to maximize. We mean to say you are literally living out the fullness of your own potential. No matter how great or how terrible your current perception of your circumstances you can thank your potential for creating the impulses that pull your existence *into existence*. Seriously.

Negative individuals are experiencing their own potential pointed back at them. Their negative potential is being maximized and they are living out the power of their own potential. They consistently create and experience negative experiences after another because they have yet to discover the disconnect between their brains and bodies. They desire good things to happen but they are compelled by impulses that lead them to the next manifestation of their potential. This is what some people call the law of attraction but it needs a little more clarification. You do not attract what you think or simply desire. Your potential is electrical and that makes you a living magnet. Potential is a form of kinetic energy transferred from brain to body and our body is literally our touch point to the world. So what you see *is* what you get.

POWER AND POTENTIAL

If you see every challenge or every inconvenience as potentially negative then it will be negative and create negative thoughts, feelings, emotions and actions. If you see that your obstacles, challenges, adversities and even inconveniences are potentially positive then they will become positive. Maybe not the experience themselves necessarily but the understanding that these things have a place in your development will increase your potential and ultimately your power to change your actions which can change your outcome.

This is important because you may still be wondering so how do I maximize potential and create power? Simply put, you maximize potential by practice. You increase your power by consistently working through all of your experiences with a mind that is set believing that *all things are working together for your good*. If you immediately went to thinking *all things are not working together for my good*, that is exactly what we are talking about. Your potential is tapped out on all the negative potential: what could go wrong, what has gone wrong, what will go wrong and the idea that everything is all wrong already.

Trained athletes utilize this concept all of the time to maximize power. As coaches and trainers we too utilize the power of potential to get our clients to achieve amazing skills and gain incredible strength that propels them into greater athleticism and confidence but it comes through repeated bouts of overcoming negative stress with the goal of making it positive stress. Although an athlete has a goal of winning you too have similar goals and their perspective can give you a great insight into what it takes to increase your power and potential.

THE FLIGHT OF YOUR LIFE

> Negative individuals are experiencing their own potential pointed back at them. Their negative potential is being maximized and they are living out the power of their own potential.

For the sake of example, when we exercise our mind sends signals that create the potential for action. You understand this but what sports practitioners understand is that with each repetition, the movement or skill becomes easier or more accessible. The more accessible the action potential becomes the less an athlete has to concentrate to make the necessary action a reality. Eventually with enough repetition, the action comes "naturally." However it was everything else but natural. For some of you that should be good news. Your potential has nothing to do with talent. It does have a greater deal to do with determination.

If you are determined to maximize your potential for the good of others and yourself then you will develop the power to create that good and move culture and your life forward, no matter how insignificant your role or vocation may seem. Your impact and your ability to do positive things to create positive engagements and interactions, will bring a whole lot of good into your life because potential is predicated upon finding the quickest or most reliable pathway to making action happen. This is a form of reciprocity. If you give of your potential to create positive propulsion you will be continually found in propulsive positions of influence and gain. After all what is power except the ability to act, to direct, influence with strength and force creating energy that can empower other people, places, or things?

Given that compiled definition from various sources it is important that we focus on the word *force*. Force is ultimately the name of the game. To increase potential is to increase force and the rate of force. Force is not necessarily

POWER AND POTENTIAL

forceful in approach although it can be. Force is also not necessarily compelling although it can be. For the sake of our discussion we want to focus on the positive position of force as an expression of the true power of potential. The greater the force the greater the acceleration. This is why sports experts often regard force as king.

FORCE IS KING

Taking flight and maximizing potential and power requires a great deal of relative force. However force is only as powerful as its application. Having the potential to produce force does not move anything but actively engaging that potential can literally move mountains. The right amount of force focused directly into another object or person at exactly the right instant can unlock a new personal best or crown a champion. The right amount of force can be instant enough to create great damage or even be fatal. Force is king but mastery is the old wise sage.

    Applied force can literally change the trajectory of a person or thing. You may have great potential but you may lack the discipline to apply that force accurately and with enough concentration to set a new personal best or to achieve your greatest level of performance in life, business or sport. Force is propulsive it changes distance, direction and velocity. Force is the potential of being intentional in the direction that you want something to move.

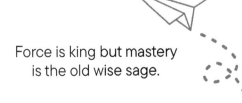

Force is king but mastery is the old wise sage.

THE FLIGHT OF YOUR LIFE

Mastering force requires an honest assessment of where you are and where you want to be then taking steps, no matter how small, toward that goal. However, how you train dictates the mechanics of these steps. This is why it is important to find a coach or mentor who can help you identify points in your process or progress where you are leaking energy. In sports these *energy leaks* take the force that we are trying to apply and redirect it into a counterproductive direction.

As performance and fitness coaches, these leaks are the first things we investigate before prescribing a plan to improve force or speed. Mastery begins with assessing deficiencies that may need correcting. Notice that we did not say strengthening. To become aware of deficiencies gives insight into what type of exercise or mobility technique might improve force and reduce the risk of injury. Energy leaks are not always the result of weaknesses and weakness is not necessarily something that is not strong. Energy leaks can also be mis-firings which can create a perceived weakness in areas of great strength. In more relational terms someone who is very resilient can be very strong but the deficiency or stiffness in the area of forgiveness can create an energy leak that reduces the amount of force they might produce to move beyond the moment. Rather than moving through their circumstance they continue to bear the burden of it.

In our profession we use movement screens and corrective exercises to address weak links in the kinetic chain. The kinetic chain is the structure that allows us to use force or leverage to create momentum in ourselves or external objects. Likewise when we address our life purpose, clientele looking to accelerate their lives and businesses, we assess the weakest link in their chain of operation to see if repairs or corrective measures are needed to restore the *integrity* of the structure. It is important that each area is up to par so that the entire system can withstand the level of force that their passion will be driving them into.

The objective of increasing force is to create movement not to simply be able to withstand whatever falls on your shoulders. Some of us have incredible potential and are strong enough to produce great amounts of force but if the mechanics or methods of using your force are all wrong, you can break a lot of things and a lot of people or end up breaking yourself. We know this is heavy but that is the point.

We are stressing this because there is nothing worse than your time coming to take the flight of your life but you have not reconditioned or restored your integrity. We often say, "the only thing that is worse than receiving the wrong thing at the right time is receiving the right thing at the wrong time." Maximizing potential and increasing force is all preparation. An athlete is unaware of exactly what he or she may encounter on any given day but they are prepared to make adjustments within milliseconds. The time is never right. In fact it almost often is wrong but the moves that you make must be ready whenever that time is.

When potential is unprepared and when the force required is greater than the force reserved, power is meaningless and humility is required. The mastery of force is also knowing where your maximum force is. This can only be explored by strategic exposure to stress. In strength and conditioning there are tests that measure our personal bests which give us benchmarks or references that we can look into to assess progress and performance. You may be familiar with some or all of these examples: the forty-yard dash, hundred-meter sprint, one-rep maximum test, vertical jump test, five-ten-five drill, etc.

If you have no idea what any of these are do not worry. In the same way that athletes and coaches use performance measures you too should have baseline measures or intentionally expose yourself to challenges or tasks that test your skill, knowledge, leadership capability or expertise. This is a very important point. Mastery requires humility and patience. It requires knowing where you are and being satisfied with creating progress which ultimately will increase to the point where you are creating and cultivating your purpose.

If you do not expose yourself to incrementally increasing challenges then you will not be prepared to make monumental gains. As mentioned, potential has the *potential* to move you forward to keep you exactly where you are or to move you backward. In order to accelerate you must initiate. You must engage yourself in activities that challenge your capacity and your capability then you must use the experience to be honest with what areas you could use a little help in. It is okay if you discover that you should absolutely give the area over to someone else to manage. That is called leadership and alignment. It is the equivalent of corrective exercises to give integrity to the chain of force. As you can eliminate energy leaks you will find more potential to apply force to other areas that you can maximize.

In some areas where you may be too strong to the point of limiting your power you may need to focus on becoming more mobile or flexible in an area that keeps you from moving at your best. We pray that you have not had to experience any physical therapy but if you have ever injured yourself, you know just how restrictive the body can become after days, weeks or months after an operation or limitation. You may even be aware of someone who recounts stories of having to gain their function or mobility all over again, maybe after an accident or operation. Immobility or a lack of willingness to change can severely inhibit potential. Typically it is a byproduct of a guard against pain or some form of suffering. Immobility can get in the way of our mechanics creating

POWER AND POTENTIAL

dysfunction in our potential by creating a protective impulse when we are in desperate need of progress.

Earlier we mentioned that the objective of increasing force is to create movement but the ultimate goal is to produce unrestricted movement that is as beautiful as it is powerful. Think of the beautiful glide of a gazelle, springbok, horse or a well-tuned runner. Have you ever noticed how they seem to float? In sprinting that is the actual objective—to be as powerful and as light as possible and to be able to put maximum force into the ground yet have maximum speed off of it. We see this in every Olympic sport the art of the form—being able to generate huge amounts of force and minimal contact time upon release and being able to repeat this over and over again.

To be able to draw upon this potential and to create the power necessary to propel your career, family and business is the reward of the disciplined who dedicate themselves to mastering their force potential and becoming one with the ability to produce huge amounts of force at exactly the right time. We have already given you a few of our secrets to increasing them both but the most important advice we can give you is to begin exactly where you are.

Maybe for you maximizing your potential means letting go of past hurts. It may mean letting go of the unforgiving-ness as we mentioned earlier. It may mean putting yourself in uncomfortable circumstances with the intentional objective to see yourself for who you truly are at this given point in time. Approach the challenges head-on and be upfront with why you want to challenge yourself and you will see great progress in potential and power.

You can also choose to invest in yourself. It may be advantageous to actually dedicate some time to improving areas of your assessed weaknesses. Contact a specialty coach if you are an athlete in need of sprinting faster. It's good if you can hit or throw but if you do not get on base or drop bombs every batting then your strengths do not give you the opportunity to maximize your potential. If you are an employee who really could use a pay raise invest a few weeks or months in that online course many of which are being given away for free through various online platforms. You can even earn accredited college degrees online for free including master's degrees!

Most importantly you may find that the area that is leaking the most is the spiritual. You may need to invest more time in conscious prayer instead of seeking the latest trend. Take time to journal and write down exactly what you want and desire to see for yourself. There is a scripture that says, "write the vision and make it plain so that he who reads it may run with it." Without a vision for yourself spiritually your ability to produce force will be limited.

As you read this your mobility may be a literal challenge. We understand that there are circumstances that can hinder us from physically moving but that cannot and will not be an excuse. Stephen Hawking lost the ability to move everything and still managed to write books, speak around the world and impact the sciences and imagination. There are literally stories of great humans with physical challenges who are truly specially-abled, have written books, starred in films, had families and lived authentic and highly impactful lives because their potential was not reduced to what they could do physically. Mentally, emotionally and spiritually, they were masters of creating huge amounts of force that continue to move industry, culture and people forward today and for generations to come.

Whatever you need to do, get up, get moving and get stronger. There are other people who are needing you to start maximizing your potential and producing massive amounts of force. So what if you have had a tough few days, weeks or years? Forgive, keep quiet, set new goals, do the work and let this be the last time that you feel this way. You may have lost a job, we get it. We have been through this as well in the past. Suck it up, quit the sulking and self-pity, take the lessons and apply them to the direction that you feel most propelled by. You have knowledge, experience and enough potential to propel your next opportunity.

In a more practical sense, write a list of jobs, functions or visions that you have for yourself. Identify the common denominator. If time or money was not an issue, what would be the path you would take? Would it be more education, more direction, more experience? Whatever it is use this common denominator as a means of exposing yourself to negative stress that will have a positive return. Create actionable steps or follow a program, give yourself a deadline and *determine your destination*. This will help you as you take control of your mastery which will increase your force. Do not be surprised if the area goes deeper than your job, role or function.

Morgan Freeman once said in a film—of course not being the first but it is Morgan Freeman. So why not? He said, "when people pray to God for patience do you think God gives them patience or an opportunity to practice patience? When people pray for love does He give them love or does He give them an opportunity to love others?" That is the power of potential. You can maximize your potential. The more you make intentional efforts to do this the more your potential will become more powerful. So powerful that others will want to give you more opportunities to practice and express your true power. Now you know that force is king mastery is the wise old sage but the person you should get to know best is the queen. She is the most powerful figure of them all. She can liberate you or destroy

THE FLIGHT OF YOUR LIFE

you from any direction. When she expresses her force you had better be on her side or out of the way. The damage that can occur from taking her for granted may prove to be the terminal edict preventing you from producing force or creating lasting momentum in any area of your life. Trust that force is king and mastery the wise man but above all else, get to know the queen and never lose sight of her. She will be your most important asset.

RECOVERY IS QUEEN

We know catchy phrases like "the blessing is in the stretching" or other nuances may seem nice. But the truth is when we reach beyond our capacity no matter how much we want a thing, we will damage ourselves, something or someone. This may have been overlooked as you read our encouragements on increasing force, potential and power. It is the secret to them all. It has been said, "behind every great man is an *even greater* woman." The same may be said concerning your attempts to push forward or to increase force. Putting yourself under stress without conscious consideration of your physical limitations can lead to failure or forfeiture. This is why we are being certain to say this to you now. If force is king, recovery is queen. This queen does not play and is not to be played with. So take her very seriously or you will not go very far or fast for long.

There is a concept in performance training and free living that stresses a work-hard-rest-harder philosophy. How well you train is only a piece of the puzzle to creating momentum and propulsion in your life. How well you recover can take what would be a gain and make it a loss. Recovery and rest have a tremendous impact

> If force is king, recovery is queen. This queen does not play and is not to be played with.

on the rate of force and peak force because the structures that are becoming damaged or programmed need time to heal and need time to lock in the adaptations that the training signals. This relates to a concept called specificity but we will go around that for a moment. Briefly if you want to get good at something, you must do the thing you want to get good at. In relationship to recovery if you want to continue to do something long enough to get good at it you must recover from doing it too excessively. Too much of a good thing is actually a bad thing.

Extensive and peer-reviewed research suggests that too much stress at high levels in training produces negative effects and decreases strength, endurance and performance. The concept is called overtraining syndrome. This syndrome is an inadequate response to excessive exercise without adequate rest, resulting in disturbances of multiple systems within the body: nervous system, hormonal systems, the immune system and emotional regulatory systems. The connection to your potential and purpose is simple. You will do well to push hard and incorporate rest and rewards into your overall plan to achieve all that you will set out to achieve. If you do not take rest seriously you will encounter burnout.

Burnout happens when we push ourselves too hard or feel like we are being pulled by every other passion or purpose besides our own. You may even be experiencing burnout right now and have yet to call it as it is. Burnout is typically accompanied by feelings of failure and self-doubt, helplessness, being trapped and defeat. You may even notice a gradual sense of detachment from your work, family or friends. If you are feeling a loss of internal motivations, becoming increasingly cynical or negative or dissatisfied then you may need to seriously consider taking a break as your first step to changing your direction. Particularly if you feel drained to the point of losing steam and self-esteem or have become dissatisfied in the area of your life that you are invested most in.

Many of our clients are surprised when they work with us and the first few weeks of their process involve detox, decompression, destressing and decluttering before we even begin taking them through purpose or performance-enhancing programming. Overtraining, overreaching and burnout are a result of not properly managing work and life stress. Not taking advantage of work-life balance not using vacation time out of fear that taking time to focus on why you are working in the first place, will somehow mark you as less professional or less committed. It is interesting how the things that we actually are committed to often get the leftovers of us when the other things are tools that were meant to help us honor the things that we are actually committed to. That is another discussion but we think you understand what we mean.

We also encourage you to become mindful of your *work-to-rest ratio*. This ratio is the basis of all performance programming and if it is not then you are either training too heavily or not heavily enough. The body functions and utilizes energy in various ways. This is where the term *energy systems* comes from. We all have three major energy systems that help us accomplish tasks and training but the significance is that each system must be trained or can only be increased within certain parameters. An Olympic sprinter would never use a five-kilometer run as part of their training to become the best sprinter in the world. That is because their selected event or sport does not rely upon the energy system that helps endurance athletes run forever. Most importantly the work and rest must correlate to the desired outcome.

If you want to get quicker but use very short rests in between attempts you would suffer a serious decline in potential, performance and power. Increasing sprint ability is contingent upon being able to maximize sprint effort with each repeat. The objective is to maximize power and output which means that more aggressive rest is needed in between efforts. The same applies to maximizing your potential across all of your endeavors. Too often we do not adhere to the principles of energy systems and think that we must always be on and always be pressing faster and faster. You may be taking on far too many projects afraid to simply speak up and ask for help.

    You would be amazed at how many clients we speak to in business who are desperately trying to stay afloat complaining that they need help but have never actually expressed that they need it to their employer. It is even worse with entrepreneurs. You may even be someone who complains to yourself, "I wish that I had an assistant," but have not made the slightest peep to your executive or supervision team because you fear that you will be seen as incapable. Truth is, there may have actually been a line item in the corporate budget for an assistant but you have taken on so much that the company assumes that you can manage even though you did not have to from the beginning. How can you expect to experience progress when you believe making real change and real progress will be punitive?

    Hard work does pay off but smart work pays forward. If you are not healthy enough to enjoy the benefits or dividends of your work then hard work will give you enough to pay off your therapy and medical bills due to unnecessary stress. Engines burn out over time and yours can too. Your goal was never to become a workaholic or someone whose largest and most significant commitment is to your work. Your work is not your identity. Your goal should be and should always reflect a commitment to your *worth*. As you begin this journey of increasing your potential and maximizing your power start

THE FLIGHT OF YOUR LIFE

looking for ways that you can incorporate rest into your days, weeks, months and long-term times of escape.

Yvana and I strongly urge you to pause, even for a day or two, before picking up the same routine and regimen. If you need to take a break then take a break. We would even suggest that you stop reading this book and step away from everything for a moment or two. Take a moment to pray, reflect, meditate and breathe. Take the initiative and prioritize your recovery. If you only tear down and never take the time to build up then you may be wasting more energy than you have convinced yourself that you are giving. Every elite person, not only athletes, are at the very least aware of the significance of healthy habits that accelerate recovery: eating habits and a balanced ratio of types of food sources, hydration, stretching and massage are all very easy to incorporate into your daily living to increase the energy that you can give to your goals.

If you are in immediate need of help or if you are honest enough to recognize that you are not the best at ensuring prioritizing rest or recovery you may need to invest in a relationship with a professional. This person can complete an occasional service check on you to ensure that you are healthy or maintaining a healthy balance. This may be a professional therapist, pastor, lifestyle or business coach, your spouse or friend who can suggest when it might be a good time to step away from work or demanding commitments.

Elite competitors have scheduled annual time away from their sport and/or training. One would think that it requires year-round training every day at the highest level of practice to overcome competitions and barriers but every legendary coach knows the best way to win is to remain healthy. It does not matter how good you are when you cannot be good when it matters. It is the same as peaking too early and missing the podium despite being the best in the world because you are hurt or over-trained. This is where the term *progressive overload* is applied. It is a means of strategically increasing volume. If your job is in a high season right now then you might need to cut back on other commitments for a short period of time and focus on getting to bed earlier. Maybe you are a parent and your children are in high season for play. You may want to commit to less travel time. Instead of making every single game choose a select number out of the season and schedule them with enough time in between that your load does not tip you into overreaching with your job or home responsibilities.

Another way that can have a more immediate impact on your work-to-rest ratio, how-

> It does not matter how good you are when you cannot be good when it matters.

ever challenging this may be for you, is to set limits to the amount of time that you give to any particular project on any given day. Some people have found great success in simply setting a cutoff time for work-related activity and set app timers on their phones to shut off notifications and/or exposure to technology at a certain point in time daily. When we used to work in the corporate structure Yvana and I would often schedule a time to turn off the lights in our office or find a dark room to escape the digital trappings of blue light spectrum and sound found in fluorescent office lighting, computers and mobile devices.

Even if you cannot afford a nap every single day these simple suggestions can, at the very least, give you back the energy that has been leaking or give you the time to recover and recharge as you prepare for another surge with greater clarity and focus. Before we move on from this point we also want to discuss another occurrence that can take place if we do not adhere to the warnings of our mind, body or spirit

THE FLIGHT OF YOUR LIFE

that something is out of balance and we continue to overreach. Remember, more effort is not necessarily the answer.

When we try to produce more than we are capable of at a given time or try to produce with more than we have left in our reserves we are forced to demand from our systems what we cannot supply. This creates a *potential disaster* waiting to happen and could lead to our injury. This is the deeper side of devaluing recovery and rest. In sports many injuries occur simply because of a lack of recovery. Many injuries occur with no direct trauma or contact. When an athlete strains or pulls a muscle typically, it is because they are pressing too hard to make something happen or ignore the sign that they have reached their current peak force or *push-and-pull relationship*. When one muscle pushes, another is being pulled or stretched under tension. There are two structures with great potential that must work together to create the necessary force to produce propulsion.

If these two do not work together in a synergistic manner they can turn from friends to enemies rather quickly. You may even have this experience in your relationships or with those you are intended to work with. This can happen when two forces work to maximize their own potential as a means of protecting themselves and lose rhythm with one another. It can also happen when one potential is far too great compared to the other that wants to stay in step but simply cannot keep up.

We have experienced both and have used these experiences to give us insight into how overreaching in our relationships can either cause unintentional damage or how being unequally yoked can lead to the failure of one of the pieces of the structure; a structure that was not as developed as we had imagined it to be and was in serious need of development before taking on the challenge that it had not been conditioned for. Some things that fall apart are of no fault of our own but may have been an expression of a lack of development on the part of someone or someplace that could not handle the level of force that your system could generate. That is a tough one to swallow but whether you were the first example or the latter, this should give you a bit of insight into yourself and your past and present relationships.

We will discuss this more in a later topic. Potential is a beautiful thing and it can lead to your progress and power but you must always be mindful that potential can also lead to problems. This is not a focus on the negative but it is a means of preparing for and staying the course if your potential creates problems when your potential propels a pattern or productivity to levels and heights that others may have not expected or seen coming.

Now that you understand a few important terms and the significance of potential and power we will take a look into the piece of power that we are after in every area of our lives, business or sport—acceleration. Acceleration is a force in itself and can be used as an expression of maximized potential and power. There are laws that govern it and we want you to be very familiar with these laws as they have some surprising insight into how you are going to prepare to take the flight of your life.

LAWS FOR LIFE

Isaac Newton is credited for having discovered the relationship between forces like acceleration and the universal laws that describe how things move or not move. If these laws are universal then that means that they can be applied to every area of creation or existence. We understand that the correlations may require a bit of imagination but imagination is genius at work. We believe that universal laws are at work externally and internally reaching beyond the scope of space and time. You may be vaguely familiar with these proposed laws but for this particular topic it is necessary that we refresh your memory. Here we'll introduce them to you so that you can gather what these laws may mean as you try to create momentum in areas of your life that will propel you to your determined destination or destiny.

Law 1: Every object will stay at rest or in constant motion unless acted on (compelled) to change by the action of an external force.

Law 2: An object's acceleration is dependent upon the total amount of force used to move the object or the mass of the object itself.

Law 3: For every action there is an equal and opposite reaction.

We can take a few great thoughts from these laws the more time that we spend connecting them to the patterns of our daily lives. That is exactly what we hope to help you do here. If you take a look at the first law you can identify that everything has a pre-purposed direction. That direction or motion is constant and will remain constant until it is no longer constant.

Your life, our lives, started on a path but along the way, we are knocked off of our original course or run into other people or objects that have an agenda or purpose that impacts the direction that we were originally headed in. We like to think of this as what we were meant to be versus who we have adapted ourselves to become. It is also known as our *ideal self* versus *ought self*. This does not necessarily mean that who you are is not who you were meant to be. In fact this is the beauty of life.

Some of us were not born into an ideal situation and are burdened by who we are likely to become if we do not encounter the proper intervention or get the appropriate push to be greater than our environment—to "make it out." Likewise, some of us are born into the ideal situation by perspective terms and are burdened by the image of who we ought to become. An incredible miniseries that speaks to this is a nonstop watch in our opinion called *Little Fires Everywhere*.

The first law expresses the significance and importance of having the right propulsors or individuals to promote us to prepare us and push us to our greater selves. It also expresses the dangers of allowing or having the improper propulsors or individuals who would rather pull us away from or push us so far away from our ideal self that we lose ourselves to who they tell us we ought to be. This is the point commonly referred to as being *in too deep*. It is not impossible to find our way back but it will be an improbable journey that will take more than we may have been prepared for to reclaim.

The second law allows us to observe the relationship between variables that we cannot control and those we can. These variables can be manipulated to increase or decrease our acceleration potential. We can choose our circles. We can choose our friends and spouse. We can choose to some degree how far or how high we wish to go and make adjustments to our lives or our bodies that can help us get there. These variables within our control can also impact how quickly or how slowly we get to the determined destination and can be changed with our own efforts.

Businesses operate on these laws heavily. In particular this one. It is incorporated into every great business and leadership structure. It is the ability to *pivot*. Pivoting simply means maximizing potential at any given crossroad where the market, demand or profitability requires a change of pace or position in order to reaccelerate or to maintain as much speed without much collateral loss or damage. Pivoting is not easy but it is what mastery is all about, as discussed in the previous topics. Mastery is being prepared for the unexpected and being able to make a split-second decision as calculated and as quickly as possible. It is the expression of agility and is a principle that sets the greats apart from the would-be great.

You are more familiar with this concept than you may think. You use it all of the time. You use it with your money. Sometimes you have it and with others you may not. You cut back where you need to in order to keep the ball moving. You use it in your relationships. If someone or something is consuming far too much time you are either going to cut back from something else or you are going to beef up on the commitments to other things so that it becomes more difficult to move your established position or plan. Athletes do the same thing. Being 350 pounds will not serve an Olympic gymnast but being one hundred pounds certainly may. What areas of your life or existence can you put more focus into and what areas can you cut back so that the influence is not too great that it controls or compels you to change your schedule or commitments?

Taking another deeper look into the second law allows us to focus on what we can control when the uncontrollable happens. It also speaks to the foresight of preparing for the uncontrollable as best we can before it comes. Yvana and I have both completed Dave Ramsey's financial freedom course. In fact we have taught it to literally hundreds of individuals saving millions of dollars and eliminating over a million dollars in debt in the course of one class. In his course Dave discusses how individuals can save for emergencies, get out of debt and then save and invest for the future. He prescribes this method to create liberty and freedom to move instead of living with debt and the fear of the unexpected looming over the heads and decisions of those he teaches.

Some of us need to consider taking control of those things which we can control instead of beating ourselves up over everything that we cannot. A bad situation can always get worse but it can also get better. We can choose what we are prepared to make happen given the choices that we make today. In the second law we can observe that if we want to increase momentum we can increase mass and force. In the case of debt Dave talks about the *debt snowball*. He often says that you must put all of your energy into gathering an emergency fund and getting out of debt as quickly as you can "with gazelle-like intensity." The intensity is referring to the force and the snowball is referring to mass. For the sake of brevity we will summarize both.

Using a debt snowball is a method of paying your highest-interest debt first until the balance is zero. Then proceeding to taking that amount that you were accustomed to and adding it to the next debt in addition to the minimum payment necessary to keep the debt current until the balance becomes zero. Then taking that new amount and repeating with each debt until there is no debt left. As time progresses momentum and mass increase into a giant snowball like the ones that you might envision rolling down the hill in the cartoons and rolling over the cartoon hero or villain for laughs and giggles.

That is only one takeaway but you may not have any debt so your mass may need to be put away long-term with various plans and policies that protect your greatest assets like Tina Turner who had her legs insured for over three million dollars. Whew! That is a joke but it's true. Consider your most valuable asset. Hopefully you were quick to realize that you are your most valuable asset before naming something that you own. Your spouse may be but again you do not actually own them, we hope. Life insurance, health insurance, disability insurance, business or liability insurance, etc.—you may even want to think about lifestyle savings otherwise known as retirement or sources of residual income. All of these are ways to prepare for the unthinkable and unexpected. If you do not get the momentum started now it may be too late to get them rolling in time. Your *savings* may not be large enough for when you need their mass to be sufficient to keep all that you have from being swept away.

There is one more truth worth extracting before moving on to the final law. That is the significance of holding on to things in areas that are actually slowing down our progress and minimizing our potential. We have touched on some of these things previously but this is worth exploring again. You may be fine financially and we truly hope that you are. You may be great competitively and we do hope that you are but emotionally and morally you may be stuck because you refuse to trim the fat or drop the excess that is keeping you from moving faster and further than you may be familiar with. Some of our greatest results are seen in clients who carry things way too tightly. We do not have to hold on to everything. Even if we have got it under control we are giving up control in areas that would be better invested in.

Some things are not worth holding on to and with respect, neither are some people or habits. We will leave that right there for a minute. Some of our potential is untapped because we have made too great of a mass out of our messes and misses. Hurt, heartbreaks or things that we are hung up on can also become energy leaks that are limiting our potential. Even holding on to high hopes and expectations of people and positions that cannot rise to the level of our vision can diminish the power of our potential and limit our propulsion. As these laws pertain to motion they also introduce us to gravity. Gravity is an acceleration that is greater than the force that we can produce. The mass to be moved is too great and keeps us right where we are because we refuse to take our hands off and let it lie. Unfortunately as we will discuss in the next coming topics, the longer we spend sitting on our potential or give energy to something that will not allow us to move, we unknowingly forfeit potential in other areas and the more difficult it becomes to make other efforts to overcome our limitation.

The third and final law coined by Newton is very unique. It directly speaks to acceleration and propulsion. It also gives us hope that everything is working together but it also puts ownership of what these forces working together will produce. For every positive there is a negative. But—and it is a big *but and I cannot lie*—for every negative there is a positive. This means that we can choose which direction we would like to go in and focus our entire existence on making that journey in that direction. This is not simply the power of positive thinking but positive living, planning, preparation, maturation and existence. It is embracing everything and knowing that we can consciously choose to see that all things move us toward our ultimate goal.

This law also gives insight into the importance of being intentional about what we put in in order to maximize what we get out. It is no different than making calculated decisions to ensure the best potential for a *return on investment*. If you want to go in direction A, you must push against direction B. You will need to consider the benefit of what negative actually means. It does not necessarily mean detrimental. It could actually mean exponential to someone whose mind is set on moving forward and upward. There is an increase in potential when you have something to push away from. This may even be why you have the circumstance that you are facing today. We do not necessarily ascribe to *what doesn't kill you makes you stronger* but if it is better worded, the

THE FLIGHT OF YOUR LIFE

phrase is an expression that some challenges come to give you the necessary friction to increase the amount of force you use to overcome or survive it.

> For every positive there is a negative. But—and it is a big but and I cannot lie—for every negative there is a positive.

Think about a swimmer pushing off of the wall to get a jump after their turn. Now imagine a swimmer making the same turn in the middle of the pool with no wall or obstacle. In our years as coaches in sports we have seen athletes compete whose blocks did not have the proper traction. When the athlete reacted to the gun they slipped immediately because all of their force went into a set of aluminum blocks and not down into the mass of the track. No matter how strong or how powerful these athletes are, they would go nowhere fast if they did not push against something. Your best option may be to stop trying to move the dumb masses in your life; instead put your muscle into pushing yourself away from it and taking advantage of the opportunity presented to you to get the much-needed leverage you have been waiting for. This will accelerate your life, vision or purpose into a new direction or back to the direction that you should have been on a long time ago.

There will always be some opposition or something large enough to pull you away from the path that you were on or should be on but your objective is to find a way to maximize potential and propulsion. Your strategy may be to let the pull think it has you just to get close enough to use its own mass against it. Sometimes you must use a pull to create the push that you need to get you back on track with greater power than you possessed, like using the edge of what could be a black hole in your path to slingshot you with greater speed than your efforts could have produced on your own.

Lastly it is important to note that the greatest achievements in life, business, health and performance would not have happened without an equal but opposite reaction or opposing force. Some of the greatest works, lives or champions would have never emerged without overcoming opposing forces. Fictional Formula 1 champion Jean Gerard said it best: "God needs the devil. The Beatles needed the Rolling Stones. Diane Sawyer needed Katie Couric." Let this be the encouragement you need to use what you are given. See everything as a means to accelerate your life, business or sports. If you do not frame your mindset in this way you risk losing the opportunity for growth and increasing potential. Do not allow what you have been given to be taken away. Life, business and sports are all very simple; use what you have or lose what you have.

USE IT OR LOSE IT

The person who has will be given more so that he or she will have *more than enough* but the one who has nothing will have even the little that he or she does have taken away.

You may be asking yourself what the statement means but there is a universal truth that is being expressed. A universal law, much like gravity, means that it has implications beyond the constructs of physics while remaining grounded and rooted in physics. The statement that you just read was a paraphrase of the *Matthew effect of accumulated advantage*. The Matthew effect can be reduced to the phrase "the rich get richer and the poor get poorer." However, that boiling down limits the fullness of the expression. The words accredited to Matthew one of the most widely known writers of the Gospels, were actually writing the words of Jesus. Although the very same principle was recorded in the writings of other disciples, namely Mark and Luke.

THE FLIGHT OF YOUR LIFE

The principle or universal law gives insight into the disparities between those who have and those who have not. However it also creates a sliver of light to look at those who would have and *those who once had*. The principle speaks beyond socioeconomic dynamics and can also reach into the science of performance and purpose. You may even have already drawn the connection to the *parable of talents* which we will discuss a few moments later but for now, we want to dive into the relationship between the principle and your ability to perform. It is important to remember that none of the principles of this book are limited to one area. Approach the next few insights with an inquisitive and creative mind.

Two thousand years predate the proposed theories of how our physical bodies respond to inactivity or lack of specific activity. Before Julius Wolff proposed his thoughts to the world of science, the concept was hidden in plain sight in the words you read at the beginning of this topic. The illustration shows how underutilization, procrastination or lack of use (sitting on your gifts or potential) can ultimately lead to the loss of ability to use or access the power once produced. You can easily correlate this to the advantages of training and preparation. Furthermore, you can draw a direct relationship of increasing levels of comfort to a lack of fire in the belly or genuine determination and grit.

This concept would later become the basis for understanding the simplicity of losing potential. Coined *Wolff's Law*, it lays the groundwork for how positive stress impacts every living thing and how no stress or negating the importance of proper stress impacts every living thing negatively. Simply put, the principle is summarized as *use it or lose it and do not abuse it*. Bones,

"live like 1st, train like 2nd."

muscles, functions and even the brain-to-body signals or potentials get weaker when not stressed *appropriately*. An easily understandable example would be the impact of having actually injured yourself to the point of needing immobilization. Yvana and I have had our share of injuries over the years. Maybe you have too.

If you have ever broken a bone or had surgery on a limb or compared limbs of others who have, you have likely observed Wolff's law firsthand. A drastic reduction in size, muscle mass or hypertrophy, strength and mobility are all signs of *atrophy*. Like your muscles, bones, tissues and skills, we do not get better the more we avoid stress. We get better the more we allow moments of pressure and create healthy stress or challenges that ultimately allow us to grow or to adapt. This principle can easily be applied to your potential in any career, endeavor or relationship. Anything that impacts our potential directly impacts our purpose or intent.

Artists who do not continually activate their gift can quickly lose their ability to perform to the same degree as they may have been able to in the past. We see the impact of Wolff's Law in everyday occurrences. You may be able to quickly recall athletes who lose their speed and power or singers who have lost their signature approach and style. Taking it into the marketplace we can also find leaders who, becoming comfortable, end up losing their influence and relationships that were not appropriately stressed or cared for and become distant memories. This is the hidden gem behind the principle. There are no guarantees even if things are going well. Taking what we have been given or, in some cases, who we have been given for granted, or as granted, is grounds for atrophy until what we had becomes the prized possession of someone else.

Yvana and I have a trademark phrase that guides the mindset of our fitness brand: "live like 1st, train like 2nd." The how he ordered his affairs. They were very familiar with the standard operating procedures (SOPs).

Imagine today, your employer, your agent or your biggest client gives you more than enough to live on for a year or more having provided no services yet but on the expectations that you, being trusted enough would do what is right with their money. After all it is still technically their money because you have not cleared the books with services rendered. Well, look at your life today. You have been given talents and have been given more than enough to get by. You may even be the classic talented individual who does the bare minimum because the bare minimum comes easy to you. You may know, coach or employ someone like this—so gifted but limits themselves because they are too talented to need to give more than what is necessary.

So as in the case with these managers, what happens when all of a sudden you are asked to give more than what is necessary? Do you quit? Do you take your talents and run? Worse, do you hide your talents because you are afraid to take a risk or to be challenged and *fake it until you make it*? Let me tell you right now the last strategy is not a strategy, it is a setup for disaster. These managers are now faced with the opportunity of a lifetime and time will always reveal those who have prayed, prepared, paid attention and put their movement where their mouth is. There will come times when you recognize just how cheap talk really can be—the time to put up or shut up.

The parable further conceptualizes the choices that each manager decides to make. One manager gets to work right away. He takes the portion that he needs to survive and thrive and invests the other portion in different streams of increase. He diversifies and remains focused. The second manager clearly sees what the first manager does and takes notes and follows suit. He may not be quite where the first manager is but he is wise enough to take a similar approach and triples what he was left with. The third manager was too taken by fear and pride. He clearly likes what the talents afford him he feels like he is on top of the world, so he begins to treat people with contempt and sees himself as having been placed above the others around him. He even convinces himself that the true owner of the talents is not returning. Worse, he is likely hoping that to be true.

As happens in life with so many who are full of potential, he becomes comfortable and assumes, when the pressure comes, "I will do what I always do and wing it." However, there's one problem—we often lose track of time when we feel that we are on top, untouchable and unaccountable. As you imagined the estate owner did return. Time had flown by and no matter how much you might think you can just spring right up and get things moving you or someone you may have observed quickly realizes that everything and everyone has moved so far along that it is impossible and improbable to catch up.

The two managers who invested in others also invested in themselves. Not only did they acquire more wealth monetarily but they also acquired more knowledge, wisdom, business sense, strategies for success, insight, potential and purpose. Not only could they manage their own estate but they also could now afford to purchase their own estate, manage it well and teach others. After giving their reports to the owner of the estate, he was so honored that instead of taking credit, he credited them with their own kingdoms! He had not only given them an advance but now he was also giving them equality and ownership. He did not even ask for the money back. Wow.

The last manager had nothing to report. He had done nothing, he had not grown and he had wasted his time and resorted to placing blame on anyone he could including the very person who had invested in him. Have you ever done this? Blamed everyone except your own decisions and lack of effort for your losses or the losses that your actions created for others? Be honest. Like this manager, you too may have lost sight of who you are, who you work for, what you were working toward or why you are working in the first place. Instead of being able to present increases in his potential or validating his potential. He had allowed his potential to die. Not fully using our potential or maximizing it creates other symptoms and syndromes in our lives: moral, ethical, and emotional atrophy. Instead of facing his fault the manager turns his anger toward the owner of the estate.

He begins to blame the owner for the lack of ability to respond to the challenge. He accuses the owner of being a thief and a hard driver deserving nothing more than what he had given the manager in the first place. What we did not disclose in the telling of this story is that the unfit manager *buried his talent.* He buried the seed and source of potential that had been given to him. He then tries to justify his actions and tells the estate owner that he should be grateful that he is getting his talent back unused. He did not even consider putting the money in the bank to earn a fraction of interest on the investment the ruler had made in him.

At the time of this writing, the world is making strides to come out of the most recent pandemic event. Unfortunately there are examples of all three managers in the lives of those who have come through on the other side of the global shutdowns. Someone went into the eighteen-month period with very little but took advantage of the time and learned a new skill, saved a little more aggressively, completed their education, started their own business, trained harder than ever before and rested harder than ever. Some people invested in their relationships with urgency and intent. Yvana and I often reference that for some, the pandemic exposed the managers who thought they would get by on their talent versus the person who was determined to invest every talent they had into something new. You may have even heard of all the millionaires made from individuals who invested in the stock market for the very first time whose status and attitude toward what is possible have changed forever. For the entire world, this has truly been the beginning of a *great reset*.

One final look at the unfit manager. Thinking that his intellect had spared him his ignorance and pride had exposed him for all that he was—a useless and untrustworthy manager who faked so hard that he fumbled. He was a coward. Some of the most talented individuals in the world are in fact afraid: cowards who are bound by a spirit of fear, false humility or arrogant pride and haughtiness or a sense of entitlement.

Here is the kicker. When we withhold our talent or do not use them, we do not commit offenses against the giver of the talent but against those who would have benefited or received from our using those talents and potential. The talents that he had received had come with no restrictions. He could have used those talents to make friends, make an impact and increase and propel himself and the lives of others forward and higher than he had ever imagined his life could have accomplished. His refusal to see how great of an impact the talents and time could have made left his life without meaning without ever tapping into his purpose or using his talent to define and *choose* the purpose he wanted to serve. He did not even have the sight to recognize those around him that he could have invested in if he had no desire to do anything with his talent. He did not teach or reach anyone. He abused and abandoned the potential of others because he had buried his own.

The manager was ruined and unbeknownst to him, had ruined the reputation of the generous estate owner, ruined the reputation of the manager's family and name, ruined the lives of those who could have benefited and ruined the relationships and the opportunity for advancement of himself and culture. He even ruined the chances of creating wealth with his talent, thinking that hiding it was the same as protecting it, thinking that leaving it unchallenged would be the smartest way to secure the bag. The estate owner was so enraged that he had the evil manager utterly destroyed. We mean, like, *whacked*.

We challenge you to assess your potential. Be honest with yourself as you look at these laws and principles in every area of your life. For you it may be health; for others, wealth, reputation, opportunities, relationships or legacy beyond where you are now. No matter where you put your potential you cannot bury responsibility. With all talents comes the *ability to respond*. Maybe like trying to skip on responsibility you skipped through the parable entirely. We challenge you to courage up and go back and give it a read here or research the parable of the talents for yourself or have our friends Alexa or Siri do it for you.

Lastly we challenge you to accept the fire you feel stirring on the inside of you and to not run from it; run with it. Your potential is priming and is ready to be expressed. Give it room and run anyway. Do it afraid, do it scared, do it and dare to defy. You will be amazed at how quickly you will begin getting the hang of it. The pressure will create a pocket around you that you can trust. Of course it is a thrill but you will find the *slipstream* made for you and a wake path that will be a guide for others who will ride on your coattails or wings.

A final word of advice before you go. Once you start do not stop moving. Always assume that there is someone behind you, trying to catch you, surpass you or stay with you. These are not always enemies. You will be creating paths to new levels for many setting records that others

> *the baton must never slow down.*

THE FLIGHT OF YOUR LIFE

will only dream to break, going a distance that many will only make because you are leading the way. Continue to move forward. Continue to move culture forward. Continue to advance and push your relationships and innovation and industry forward. When your time comes to pass the journey on, to hand the baton over, let it happen at your best at maximum speed. You do not have to slow down. In fact, that is the number-one rule of any relay: *the baton must never slow down*. So whatever you do, do not stop. Just keep pushing forward until you run into someone ahead of you whom you can pass it on to.

DO NOT STOP

As you begin to come into a greater awareness of your ability to propel not only yourself but others who will be inspired by your journey, you may encounter increased atmospheric pressure and turbulent activity on your way to more. You may be no stranger to this and the events and challenges that you have had to face in the open have created in you a hesitation as you ponder taking this all-effort attempt at the flight of your life. In times past you would see what you wanted. Having experienced failure before, you have defaulted to halting your progress and eventually slowing down completely rather than pushing ahead full throttle even if it means full-throttle intensity toward the next determined destination.

If you have ever flown on a commercial airline when a pilot senses or experiences rough air, the pilot adjusts his elevation or makes a maneuver but never does the pilot cut off the engines and completely halt propulsion. The pilot is skilled in making necessary adjustments that may not require flight at the same level in order to reach the determined destination. There are periods, some more brief than others, where you may not feel like you are where you want to be. But that is the wrong approach. Your focus should only be on making progress toward that determined destination. It is not always necessary to remain on the same level or to be on the highest level in order for you to be working toward the determined destination. There may be seasons in your life where you are not performing to the level that you desire but you cannot stop. There may be seasons that leave you running dry but you cannot stop. There may be seasons that you literally cannot take flight but that does not mean that you stop making progress in other improvements and necessary repairs. There will always come a time where your number is called and you must be ready to fly even if you have not done so in a while.

As a champion athlete for the University of Mississippi I can recall an experience on the track that has stuck with me since that day. It taught me a great lesson about life during relay hand-off practice. In the relay events athletes incorporate marks on the track to give indication for the proper acceleration timing to maximize propulsion and baton movement. The athlete receiving the baton has one primary job—to maximize their acceleration. The athlete who is passing the baton forward has one job and that is to never back off the accelerator. During this particular practice one of my team members was to receive the baton, but upon reaching maximum speed, he could not sense his teammate behind him and tried to stop his momentum in order to allow his relay partner to catch up.

As this athlete began to explain why he tried to stop it was at this point the entire team knew that was a big mistake and we all learned a lesson about our coach and about ourselves. Our sprint coach blew a gasket and threw his hat to the ground as there are typically two things a track coach has access to throw—either their hat or the stopwatch because the shades are far too expensive. The entire team

THE FLIGHT OF YOUR LIFE

stood still as the lava began to flow from our coach's veins to his words: "slow down...No, you speed your —— up! Don't you ever —— tell him to slow down. It's your job to sprint all the way through the zone. If he can't get there then it is his fault. You do not stop. The baton must never slow down. Now get your —— back to that mark and run through the exchange!" Then he turned to the athlete who did not sprint with all of his effort in order to be on the mark as rehearsed. Needless to say, their next hand-off was dead-on.

    We have no doubt that you will make progress as you focus toward maximizing your potential and your power but that does not mean you will not have moments of doubt. We also have no doubt that you may also be terrified once you begin seeing progress being made so rapidly and face the temptation to dial back your own acceleration. If you are serious about losing weight you cannot stop this time. The flight of your life is life or death. If you are going to set a new personal record you cannot stop until you see a record time. The flight of your life is about continual improvement. If you are going to create your own business, write a book or invest in some relationship, you cannot stop once you get started. The flight of your life is loss or legacy.

    We understand that there are circumstances that we cannot prepare for but that does not mean that our flight is over. I underwent open-heart surgery and two other heart surgeries during high school. I also had a dream and an absolute conviction that I could compete at a division 1 program. I was determined to get there and embraced that this was the way I had to go to get there. I sat out an entire year, became a team manager for basketball and eventually returned to competition as a sophomore. I made it to state but I did not win. I had my last heart surgery and came back junior year with a mission to medal. I made it to state and medaled in my event. I decided to play basketball and was actually showing a lot of skill then I strained a groin muscle. I resigned from basketball immediately with these words: "I am leaving because I am going to run track in college on a scholarship." I not only ran myself into the record books, I became a state champion ranked among the top in my event nationally and signed a division 1 scholarship. You would think the road got easier but it never does. I would spend my first year battling injury until I was redshirted for the outdoor season. The coaching staff had even considered transferring me to a smaller program at one point but Coach Joe Walker saw what I saw in myself and we committed to making me a champion and it worked.

I had not finished any higher than sixth in the SEC and had never qualified to compete for an NCAA National Championship. In my last year I won the SEC championship title. I strained a hamstring but still managed to place in the top three in the East region. All I had ever wanted to do was to compete for a national championship. Although I was not healthy enough to defend the seed I entered the national championship in, I finished that season ranked in the top five in the NCAA overall and top twenty overall in the United States among all competitors—amateur or professional.

As you might have imagined I continued to train as an Olympic hopeful in 2008 while working a full-time job in marketing. That year I attempted to make the leap professionally only to suffer a ruptured Achilles in my very first competition as a transitioned athlete. I was hurt a little but by this time the lesson had been ingrained in me. Do not stop. A few weeks later I volunteered as a track coach and began to pass my knowledge forward to youth in my community. Many of those athletes became state champions. Then I began assisting at a local college and in the first year of a new program we finished in the top of our conference with fewer than twelve athletes. We even had one unanimously clear athlete-of-the-year recipient. My work later helped grow an academic awareness program that helped struggling student-athletes to meet NCAA eligibility qualifications. I was honored to mentor, coach and guide many athletes who would later compete in the highest level of sports nationally and internationally. Some of whom are undisputed future Hall of Famers. The techniques I learned in goal setting, vision and mission. Establishing a plan of purpose and accountability would become the foundation of the system that Yvana and I now use in our purpose coaching and consulting business. Eventually every institution of learning would benefit from the work that my colleagues and I had done to make a momentous change that would level the field for academics, athletics and advancement in my home state.

Yvana is no stranger to success or surrender. She excelled in the hurdles as a high school athlete and was ranked among the top in the United States. She was sought after by some of the most powerful programs in the NCAA. Yvana, who would finish in the top five at the high school national championships her senior year, had also been running with pain so severe in her shins that she could not walk without assistance after competition. She continued to press through as her condition was thought to be nothing more than shin splints a common inflammatory response to the rigors of run training. Her ultimate desire was to compete at a Division I program in the state of Florida. She had rejected other secure offers because she had an unwavering belief that a Florida school would reach out to her by the time she had graduated, as it happened. Yvana inked a full scholarship with the University of Southern Florida and was on her way to what had been, at that time, her greatest dream.

As she began training at USF her pain increased to the level that required another look. Her new sports medicine team x-rayed her shins to find that she had been running on two fractured tibias. The fractures were deep into her marrow and threatened to end her dream before it had begun. The prescribed treatment was to surgically repair the damage by hammering metal rods into her tibias and having them screwed in to secure the fractures. She was told that she would be confined to a wheelchair for a year and would require intense therapy. Furthermore her scholarship was absolutely in jeopardy. You can imagine how devastating this would be to a sixteen-year-old child. Yes Yvana began college as a sixteen-year-old who was talented enough to compete nationally and intelligent enough to receive top marks academically.

Yvana's mother is a praying woman and she refused to accept the news. The coaching staff and team trainers were pushing Yvana to have the surgery but she opted to accept a medical redshirt instead. Her mother prayed with Yvana daily for healing and repair as Yvana would continue therapy and homeopathic supplementation to aid her recovery. A year later both tibias had healed with greater density than before and she was cleared to compete again. Yvana would run a university record in her event surpassing a mark left by one of her greatest *inspirations* and Olympian, Damu Cherry-Mitchell. Off the track Yvana made the dean's list and was nominated by USF Athletics as a nationally recognized nominee for the NCAA Female Athlete of the Year. That same year in the hot Louisiana sun in April of 2007 Yvana and I met at a track competition. We just so happened to be sitting beside each other. That very day I knew that she was going to be my wife and I was willing to do whatever I needed to do to make that happen. Four years later we were married to each other—on three separate occasions. We hope that you better understand why it is imperative that

THE FLIGHT OF YOUR LIFE

you do not stop. You have no idea the story you are writing to be passed on that will propel your life and that of others.

That is only the beginning. A few other momentous accomplishments for Yvana was being able to take advantage of the redshirt year to earn a master's in physical education, competing for a USA national championship, qualifying for the 2014 Olympics and winning a Bahamian national championship. A working actress, Yvana was cast to portray one of the greatest boxers in history in an international commercial. She serves as a mentor and coach to athletes and individuals at all levels of life and sport. She travels internationally as a global presenter for one of the largest luxury vehicle brands in the world. She is also co-CEO of our personal and performance training brand.

We hope that our stories help emphasize the power of potentiation and how important it is to maximize force and potential. We are flattered if somehow we impressed you but our goal is to inspire you. We want to push you forward. We are very humbled to look back over all that we have accomplished this far. The lives we live create dreams in others. We are living the adventure. We are taking the flight of our lives creating momentum for ourselves and others. As you recall your own story take time to identify how one step led to another. That should give you confidence that even if the end result was not ideal it is only part of the story. You can choose to be pulled deeper into the level of dissatisfaction and disappointment or you can begin to rely on *the goal* that will propel you so fast that you take every experience and use it to create change and influence in your spheres of influence. If you have yet to fully comprehend, propulsion is the expression of power. Look for things that push you forward, the things you are willing to push for or to be pushed to achieve.

> propulsion is the expression of power.

CHAPTER 4

Potential and Problems

As you work to increase your potential, you will likely experience problems that present themselves on account of your increased potential. *Potential problems* may come in the form of delay, disappointment, missed or dissed opportunities and unexpected challenges and challengers. In video games there is a known rule regarding leveling up in potential. As your skills increase and your proficiency increases so do the challenges, obstacles and challengers. Rap artist Andy Mineo said it this way, "what did you expect, once you level up, don't you know the boss gets bigger?"

The potential problems we are discussing are not those that come because you do not have enough but rather because you are capable of more with your increasing potential. You would expect the greater the potential the easier life or success would come but it is never that way. It is the last tenth of a second that is hardest to reach, the last ten pounds, the pay raise you feel you deserve, the position, the lead role, etc. The CEO of a company makes the most money but he or she does not necessarily have the easiest job or the least stress. Their potential *is* great but the challenges get greater.

    How you handle these potential problems can have the greatest impact on exactly how high and far-reaching your potential may take you. It is very important to take an account of and to prepare for potential problems by having a go-to plan of action. You must think like a veteran pilot, flight attendant, air marshal or any other role or function that assists in exigencies. These external structures like our peers, families or the structures in which we work can take issue with your pursuit of increased potential. As you challenge yourself you by nature are challenging the external status quo or predictable expectations of your current level of expressed potential. On the other hand you must also think like the maintenance and repair technician whose work often goes unnoticed but prevents many of the unforeseen problems that could arise on account of expressing one's full potential. A jet has the potential for high speed but if unchecked, something as small as an electrical problem could prove destructive despite the potential.

    This is why we are stressing that your internal components receive extra care. If internal components are damaged or function improperly your flight could become detrimental despite your potential. Take a moment to consider your internal components: attitudes, beliefs, and perceptions about yourself and others. Take time to consider a safety measure that you can put in place or hire someone whose job it is to call you out on these areas that could prove detrimental to your progress if left unchecked. For instance potential problems can be magnified if there are flaws in your accepted reality or *personal reality*. Things like pride, arrogance, bigotry, inferiority or superiority complexes may give rise to potential problems that manifest themselves with external consequences. If you are not sure where to

POTENTIAL AND PROBLEMS

start, start with asking those who know you best what they may see that you are unaware of but it will require humility in order to find the peak of your potential.

Pilots undergo years of training and various simulations in preparation for potential problems despite their knowledge and experience. Many are trained military pilots who may have toured or flown in the heat of conflict. These men and women are trained to engage their senses and instincts and yet must continually learn how to fly in conjunction with updated electronic instrumentation that relays unbiased data, feedback and performance indications. If a pilot were to rely solely on his or her instinct, the risks would be unthinkable and the likelihood of being misled or completely missing the mark increases exponentially despite their potential. This is the same for us all as we seek to improve our potential without considering the weight and full responsibility of that potential.

Internally potential problems create misguided perceptions of how we see ourselves, our surroundings and our relationship between either. These types of potential problems can cause us to miscalculate our approach and can even cause us to do more damage than good as we enter tunnel vision on reaching our highest point without considering our impact on the ascent of others. The higher we climb, the greater our biases can be and the more disoriented or distorted our perceptions can become. Learning to rely upon unbiased instrumentation—our faith, our core values and the influences of others with our best interests at heart like our spouse, significant others and even children—can help us keep our heads while in the clouds as opposed to keeping our heads in the clouds. Having these people in place can give us a clearer and unbiased indication of who we are, where we are and how we are actually doing in our journey. The most crucial aspect of these instruments is their

THE FLIGHT OF YOUR LIFE

ability to reduce our risk to falling into the downward spiral of distraction.

On the other side of distraction is often destruction. Distractions are always around. You may recall this from our earliest discussion on call to action. Not everything that seeks our attention is intent on helping us maximize our potential. We are all susceptible to being pulled away from our focus and being compelled to entertain artfully crafted misdirection, misperception and misinformation. We live in the media millennium that feeds us images that increase our capacity for compulsion. These devices are designed to create division between our purpose and our focus. They create an addictive indulgence through imagery and illusion that is very effective at pulling us out of the flight path we belong convincing us to strive for what does not belong or pertain to us. You may be facing the challenge of discerning how much of your life is being lived through the latest social media filter versus that which is being experienced through the filter of the flight of your life. These platforms are effective at intentionally compelling us distracting us to alter our direction as we slowly drift off course from our determined destination.

There is also a great risk of losing sight of what we are truly after. Losing sight of the ultimate reason that you became determined to take the flight of our life in the first place is sad. The problem that can occur with potential is losing a connection with our *why* even if for a moment that moment could be long enough to totally cause us to miss what we were made for. Texting while driving, scrolling while driving—one movement of distraction has caused many a crucial missed step or blinded turn that proved more costly than ever expected. This is why it is imperative to be brutally honest with oneself to assess potential problems within us that could cost us all that we are working so hard for.

POTENTIAL AND PROBLEMS

A very close team member of mine experienced this firsthand. Mike was a stud at the University of Mississippi. He competed in track and had entered the secret service shortly after graduating. Only a few years into his active service Mike was in a terrible accident. A pedestrian made an illegal turn into oncoming traffic as Mike was cruising on his patrol motorcycle on duty in Washington. He was critically injured and spent time in the ICU hanging on to his life. A newly married man with a child on the way and suddenly something so drastic impacts his life. Upon further investigation CCTV video released from the intersection shows the driver was distracted as she was engaged in a text-message conversation. She had also been driving with a suspended license. That one movement of distraction cost her freedom and fines and almost cost the life of one of the nation's greatest individuals. Period. It almost cost the life of a loved teammate, son, husband and father.

You may recall stories of great individuals with so much promise and purpose whose lives and impacts were cut short by potential problems of their own making. I once read a social media post that said, "I am here for a good time, not a long time." Yes life is good and good times are excellent experiences but the problem with potential is living to maximize good times can lead us down the path of our own destruction. There will be many good moments in the flight of your life but you must not allow them to take the place of purpose. Good moments and good people are a part of the journey but losing sight of where these belong can compel you to chase them over purpose. It is up to us to keep these in their proper seat in the flight of our lives. Seemingly innocent temptations and illicit opportunities will present themselves on account of your potential. The warning is simple: potential problems will arise within us and around us. Take an honest assessment of areas unchecked and put the proper safety mechanisms in place before pushing the control or yoke forward.

    Check your motives, be honest with your struggles and temptations, keep an eye on your attitude and use discernment when engaging outside entities. Such entities would want to get out in front of you and redirect your path and at all cost, avoid distractions. Protect yourself from becoming a statistic by focusing on living a story worth telling. Define your own success but do not let success be your potential problem. Plainly we are not necessarily talking about money. There are individuals who have become very successful at things that are keeping them bound or holding them back. There are individuals that have become comfortable with never maximizing their potential or that of others. They are still a success but in the negative sense of the word. Contrary to what you may agree with some people go to bed feeling accomplished because they did something that felt *good to* them that was not actually *good for* them. We are not making light of challenges, addictions and the truth of struggles that all individuals may face. We are discussing the significance of taking account of things that may seem good but are detrimental to the desired outcome and intentional purpose of our lives.

    There is a powerful scripture that says, "Everything is permissible but not everything is beneficial." Some things are not a question of legality but a question of leverage. Whether for our good or our destruction success, like the universal laws we discussed in chapter three, can be positive or negative in result despite being 100 percent expressed. Success is amoral but we are not. Success is an expression of who we are not what we have. It will expose what has always been in us like the Parable of the Talents. This and a few other topics we will discuss will cover potential problems. As expressed in the examples we began this chapter with some potential problems come despite you doing everything right and doing it as committed as you can.

We hope that this discussion means as much to you as those preceding it. Do not avoid uncomfortable or challenging things. Remember you are choosing propulsion over compulsion. Continue to read forward as we discuss potential problems within ourselves and our environments and a few strategies on how you may continue to ensure that you are propelling forward.

> Everything is permissible but not everything is beneficial.

ATTITUDE AND LATITUDE (FREEDOM)

You may have heard the phrase, "your attitude determines your altitude." That is not a complete thought technically. In aviation, *attitude* is our relationship with earth and is visually reflected in the relationship of our nose and wings to the horizon. Attitude directly affects performance. Attitude plus power equals performance. Without the appropriate attitude our performance will suffer, and so will we. Before leaning toward the obvious it must be interpreted that there are times when changes in attitude are appropriate given the circumstance in which power or performance must increase. Ultimately it is more important to master these variables in order to ensure that propulsion does not decrease.

Although we are great fans of the coined Zig Ziglar quote we have come to understand that altitude does not necessarily reflect freedom, latitude does. Latitude gives degrees of freedom in action and thought. It is indicative of liberty, space, independence, play and unrestricted access. Latitude is equally important in taking the flight of your life. If going upward is the only goal then the goal is missed. Going higher is an aimless goal if you are not making every attempt to reach further than ever imagined. One of our favorite prayers to reference is that of Jabez. He simply asked that God would bring the change that he needed. He wanted nothing more than to enlarge his territory. This meant that his ultimate desire was to have a greater reach and impact that would ripple far beyond him and beyond his life. That should be the goal. That is the truest measure of performance. Instead of looking to maximize altitude consider the significance of latitude. Latitude is legacy. Attitude determines altitude *and* latitude.

If this is the case then there must be ways to ensure that the appropriate attitude is presented at the right time and reason. Aviators use instruments called *attitude indicators* to keep level. In life attitude indicators can keep us from banking too far left or right, can give us an aligning reference to keep us on track and can help us maneuver with confidence when distractions or potential problems arise. There is a caveat that must be considered, as you might expect, with any piece of signaling equipment that impacts our relationships both structurally and externally. Attitude indicators can malfunction when not properly cared for or if neglected. They are sensitive to impacts whether we make the impact or something else does. If not careful, we can disturb the degrees of freedom that allow them to operate correctly. So it is imperative that we check the calibration of relationships with others who serve as our external attitude indicators as well as the attitude indicators within us. Just as it is important to maintain our internal core components it is imperative that we are attentive to and properly care for our valued relationships. Those individuals whose love for us serves as attitude indicators or that help us adjust, deserve care that ensures the maintenance of their role or function in our lives.

POTENTIAL AND PROBLEMS

Looking at the other side of the coin attitude indicators give insight into our inner working parts, the systems that give us our instinctive responses. As you commit to increasing potential and maximizing the flight of your life we encourage you to take ownership of these mechanisms that may have been given to you. You may come to find as you question yourself that you have accepted and embraced opinions—whether personal, political or passed down—that were handed to you that have left you out of balance and in desperate need of calibration. For you this may even be the true reason that each attempt you have made to take the flight of your life ends before it begins.

Attitude determines altitude and latitude.

Your attitude indicators if not maintained, can become stuck leaving you to believe that you are flying level despite the fact that your wings are not in alignment with who you need to be. You may have seen vehicles like this on the road. The steering wheel is straight but the vehicle is driving out of alignment and the rear end is shifted so far to one side that the car looks like it's driving sideways but going straight. If you are not in proper alignment with who you need to be right now in order to become the person that you desire to be then your efforts are in vain. You will break something before you get there. Although we are talking about maximizing potential the truth may be that you do not need any more power to take the flight of your life. You may just need to revisit the things that were meant to correct your course.

THE FLIGHT OF YOUR LIFE

We challenge you to step outside of yourself for a moment and push back the notion that you were "made this way." To rest in the statement "this is the way that I am" is a cop-out based on compulsion. Whoever you choose to be is who you will remain to be. Just bear in mind that whatever we choose forfeits what we would become. You should understand that you may certainly be a product of your environment, but the sum of these parts can be changed by who and what we add or subtract to the equation. Sometimes that means in order to maximize our true potential, we cannot afford to keep ourselves padded by things or people that we agree with on every level. That actually has the opposite impact on our potential and we will find comfort as we conform.

Challenge yourself and look deeply with a critical eye at your beliefs, political views, clubs and associations. Do you see patterns of inferiority or superiority? Do you see discriminatory biases intentional or unintentional? Are you someone who feels entitled or can you see how others might perceive this message? Be open enough to think of how these things have impacted your family, your career, your team or your goals. Have you accomplished them all? Have you been let go justifiably? Did someone end a relationship with you? If any of these questions trigger an initial thought that was anything other than propulsive and you felt offense, ask yourself why. If the purpose of this book is to push you to identify areas that could be limiting your potential question why some of your own questionings lead you to feel disturbed.

As you come to understand the significance of attitude as it pertains to flight it makes sense to embrace that your attitude indicators may need servicing. If they only serve to confirm that you are always right then you are not aligned with your long-term goal or the ultimate goal for your life has not been properly determined. You may think that you are

POTENTIAL AND PROBLEMS

choosing your direction but your own devices may compel you to fly further away from where you really need to be. Again this is not a knock on your convictions. These are different and we will discuss them later on. However we are challenging you to allow others with differing viewpoints to help you better align yourself with a vision of purpose rather than a particular party or program.

As a word to your wisdom it would benefit you greatly to keep those around you who do not always agree with you or see things the way that you do. Do not remove or attempt to repair individuals who may actually be flying in balance. They may have completed the work of maintaining their attitude indicators and are not compelled by your personal views. These are people who should be in your view. They can offer you another vantage point. Like a good attitude indicator these individuals can serve as references when your attitude indicator has been damaged or impacted by forces that disturb its degrees of freedom. If you need to have relationships that you can control or manipulate, keeping them on your terms or timetable, then your attitude indicator will continue to malfunction.

This is a very sensitive issue for most of us especially if we need to deal with arrogance, entitlement or egotistical biases that view other people as beneath us or under our authority mentally or spiritually. It is not uncommon to avoid people who challenge us or to not take kindly to those that God will send into our lives to expose these injurious biases so that we could become free and maximize our potential and power. If you are someone who cuts everyone out of your life who does not particularly agree with you or look like, love like or live like you do then you are likely trying to navigate the flight of your life with a damaged or broken attitude indicator.

THE FLIGHT OF YOUR LIFE

Like a vehicle that needs an alignment after driving around long enough the misalignment feels normal. I recall in graduate school learning of how excellent our minds are at making adjustments. In particular I remember reading of an experiment by Professor Theodor Erismann and discussing an experiment where his pupil Ivo Kohler, was given optical glasses that inverted his sight. After wearing the eye coverings for approximately ten days Kohler had adjusted and his brain had decoded the visual discrepancy and corrected his sight. What was down had now become what was up. Despite having the world manipulated through reflections in tiny mirrors within the glasses that painted the world upside down, Kohler's brain had accepted the bias and made corrections automatically.

Just like the corrections made automatically by the glasses our attitude can make these adjustments in how we approach the world and others in it without our being aware. Unfortunately flying on autopilot does not necessarily mean that you are safe. You may be in a downward spiral and just haven't been made aware. That is the worst potential outcome associated with potential problems—being on a downward decline thinking that you are flying high. This is known in aviation as a graveyard spin.

A graveyard spin is typically entered into unknowingly. It can occur when flying *through* storms or disturbances that cause low visibility (i.e., the dark of night). Without reference to the horizon or experiencing an attitude indicator malfunction, we lose orientation and fly with a wing bias. What makes this phenomenon unique is that the same adjustment in our brain that was observed in the before-mentioned experiment occurs here. We are fully aware that something is not right but our equilibrium adjusts and tells us that our bias is completely balanced and right side up and we set our wings at the angle which is most comfortable. Our own equilibrium leads us to believe that we are cruising until we notice that we are not going up but approaching the ground. Logically, in an attempt to escape this inevitable crash, we pull back on *the yoke* which does not change our directions but tightens the spiral and increases the speed of our downfall.

If this topic scares you or makes you a little uncomfortable we are giving you the courage to face and embrace the possibility that your attitude needs adjusting. Maybe you do not need change in the way that you expect or have been compelled to believe by the manipulation of the insincere or insecure around you. That is a potential problem that does occur as you take back your authority and ownership of the flight of your life which we will discuss in coming pages. Choose today to reclaim your degrees of freedom.

You do not have to continue the downward spiral that may have been set in motion by hurts or even those with good intentions who misled you at an early age to believe flying left or right was the way to fly straightforwardly. Resolve within yourself to repair those places where damage from experiences or individuals left you immobilized or impaired. Forgive them then choose to move forward. Forgive and fix it. Like my mother Annie D. Campbell would tell me as a young man, "there are some things in life you do not need to pray about. You already know what *you* need to do."

BELONGING IS BELIEVING (FAITH)

It is worthless to take the necessary steps toward the flight of your life only to forfeit the moment of opportunity those steps have afforded you. This is a potential problem. Lacking a sincere belief that you belong may be the basis of a self-sabotaging mechanism. Not believing that you belong has real-life consequences. It is compelling enough to convince you that you will fail even before you begin. You will never find yourself in the place that was made for you with this thinking because it is powered by a genuine faith in your failure. Nelson Mandela said, "one cannot be prepared for something while secretly believing it will not happen."

You will never take hold of your determined destination while holding onto the belief that you are not worthy of the power or possibility of your potential. It matters not how many times you have tried or failed. If there is a knowing on the inside that you possess the potential for greater then you will always feel unfulfilled until you begin to rethink your narrative. Put your hands on the yoke, take ownership of your vehicle of purpose, find a new frame of reference on the horizon, shift your attitude and put all of your effort into a direction and watch the level up. This is what we call having a new y*oke* state of mind. It is putting yourself in propulsive positioning. Propulsive positions occur where propulsive faith, propulsive thought and propulsive action meet.

Propulsive position means being next in line for takeoff. At that point there is no turning back. You have committed. You belong. You are committed to creating a new reality. Whatever that may be you are geared up or fed up and at the first sign of clearance, you are asking no questions. You see your opportunity and you are seizing it. You are no longer going to step aside as others take the flight of their life. You are no longer going to accept excuses as to why you were not in position in the past. You are in your seat and you are not giving it up for anyone. You know that you belong exactly where you feel connected most and that is living life in complete freedom. You are choosing propulsion and you will stop at nothing and be stopped by no one. You have no contingency plan. You are planning to go as hard as necessary to go as far as possible. Whether anyone cares to support or not is none of your business. You have made up your mind that your dream or your goal is as good as yours. This is when you truly know that you believe that you belong.

This level of freedom and faith will cause opportunities to come into place. People that were not even aware of you will begin to pay attention. Teams, companies, investors, friends, family and even potential companions will see that you are serious and will thrust you into environments that you once believed were only the elite. Almost suddenly you may be thrust into the company of others who have accomplished, experienced or achieved what you have only imagined. Being in propulsive position will put you in meetings, boardrooms or networking opportunities with those who others would consider to be greater than you. Yet their attention is on you. If you have ever seen the show *Shark Tank* then you understand what putting yourself in propulsive position can do. It can accelerate you to a room worth billions and literally have some of the most wealthy individuals in the world fighting for the chance to propel your potential even further.

It is also to be noted that the difference between those who propel even further and those who do not is as simple as believing they belong. Pastor Keion Henderson said, "those who are great know they are great because they can walk into a room full of great people and not be moved or intimidated." In other words they have partnered with the propulsive power within them given by God. When you know that the power that is in you came from an original source that is bigger than your past and your present that should give you great confidence to continue moving forward because your entire existence and meaning is wrapped in your propulsion.

Wherever you stand you exist. You belong wherever you believe you should be. Period. You need no further validation or confirmation, you need dedication to see it through. No matter who or what compels you to believe otherwise establish within yourself this foundational truth: "I belong."

THE FLIGHT OF YOUR LIFE

> Wherever you stand you exist. You belong wherever you believe you should be. Period.

Wherever you are, you belong. No matter where life propels me *I belong*. No matter what I had to go through to get there *I belong*. No matter who had to let go of me for me to go *I belong*. No matter how grand the responsibility *I belong*. No matter who else thinks they deserve to be where I am *I belong*. No matter who thinks I should not be here, *I am,* and…I *belong*.

This must be concreted into your soul as you will encounter this potential problem on the flight of your life. Begin embracing new environments, circles and atmospheres. The words "I belong" are two of the most powerful tools in your prepared safety kit. When you are asked or may even ask yourself why you are so determined to reach the places meant for you your only answer should be "I belong."

You do not have to see it to believe it. That is the essence of faith. It is the only evidence of what is not yet seen. It is the very substance of the things that you have hope for. It is all the proof and fuel you need. The greater the proof the greater the combustibility. *Faith is fuel for forward. Faith is fuel for forward. Faith is fuel for forward.* The centralized belief that you belong will keep you in flight when your sense of belonging does not match your experience. When the potential problem of feeling worthless, insignificant or inferior arises, you will have the fortitude to keep moving forward. Believing that you belong is a declaration of faith that will keep your attitude in line and keep you free to make maneuvers that may save your life and many others. Faith is the secret to having ice in your veins. Faith will keep you in proper reference of who you are in relationship to who you are becoming.

Faith will serve as a fire that keeps your flame burning when no one knows your name or understands your vision,

POTENTIAL AND PROBLEMS

service, skill, product or idea. Faith will keep you waking up each morning determined to work toward a direction that no one else can see. Faith will keep you humble in glory or gain. Faith will keep you focused in moments of loneliness, lowliness or loss. Those who believe that they belong are faith-full, hope-full and force-full. To be faithful is to be loyal, constant and steadfast. To be hopeful is to be inspired and optimistic about the future and are likely to succeed. To be forceful is to be strong, assertive, vigorous and powerful.

May this be the last season that you limit your capability. It is honorable to give honor to others but it is a disservice to not honor that which is already within you. Choose to no longer believe that you are not knowledgeable enough, pretty enough, talented enough, educated enough, light-skinned enough or any other form of not enough. Enough with that! You are more than enough. Open the windows of your soul and allow people to see you then leave them to deal with that. All that you are in any moment is all that you ever need to be. Believe that you belong and have the faith that you are made for more. It is this propulsive thinking that will accelerate you into your greatest adventure, your best living. No matter the environment or challenge—win or lose—when the dust settles you will be where you need to be.

Believe that you belong. Strengthen your self-worth and self-validation. You are worthy of the flight of your life. You are worthy of increase, of platform, of impact, of life change and of a life that creates change. Fill your circle with others who believe that not only do you belong but they do too. If the people in your circle do not believe that you belong the circle you will find is not a circle but a cord that binds you to the status quo keeping you from maximizing your potential and propelling yourself into the flight of your life.

THE FLIGHT OF YOUR LIFE

ONLY BELIEVERS BELONG (FRIENDS)

When I first began coaching Yvana professionally I remember running into the strength coach, the former world champion hurdler David Oliver, at a local gym. In our conversation we began discussing track and field and I mentioned that I was coaching my wife. He asked me things like her resting heart rate and other relative performance measures then he asked me one final question. He asked, "does your wife believe that she belongs?" The question would become a centerpiece of mental training with Yvana but it impacted *me* far greater as a coach.

I certainly believed that Yvana was a champion and I believed that she deserved to compete against some of her heroes but I had not asked myself the question. Did I truly believe that *I* belonged as her coach? At this point in my career I had never coached another semiprofessional or professional athlete besides myself. I had coached several high school and collegiate athletes to winning championships but this was a different level. This was also *my* wife and this was *her* dream. I volunteered to coach her without having any facilities or any financial resources at that time. I had left my job to be with her and then we began talking about championship goals. What made me audacious enough to believe that I could coach her? She had been invited to train with a world-class coach at a world-class facility but we did not have world-class money at the time. So we were convinced that we could do this together.

The adventures that we have lived have been astonishing. We did not reach the Olympics but we came so close—like "winning a National Federation Championship" close and having your name at the top of the list for a country to send you to represent a people on the biggest stage in athletic competition. It is one of those things that can only be communicated this way: I believed in her and I believed also in me. We believed in each other. If I did not share this sincere conviction that she belonged and I too belonged, I would have been holding her back. We could always wonder if someone else may have helped her along further but at what cost? The woman that she is today amazes me every day. Yvana is not an old athlete whose identity is still wrapped up in the glory years. Not only did we maximize her potential as an athlete we maximized her life potential as an individual.

This is a typical potential problem with our talents. It is difficult to find people who want more for you than the obvious those who are willing to sacrifice with you and are fearless enough to endure the flight with no guarantees. If you are going to take the flight of your life your inner circle must be composed of those who have your back in such a way that maximizing their potential pushes yours forward with it and vice versa. If there is someone in your life that you share this with this is your family. Family believes that you belong and believes that they belong in your life also to see that you take the flight of your life and who feel that the further they can propel you the further they will be propelled.

If you are holding onto relationships with even the most well intentioned you must be sure that they are not limiting your propulsion because they do not believe in their ability to propel you forward. If an employer, a mentor, pastors, relatives and friends genuinely believe that you belong but cannot say the same for themselves, despite their strongest desire to aid your propulsion, it is not uncommon for their lack of belonging, fear of failure or insecurity to limit the propulsive power in your life. It is important to seek intimate knowledge of those we place our trust in as they can also become challenged by our ambitions or abilities. As a means to prevent us from jettisoning the relationship some of our closest relationships would rather keep us manageable within arm's reach.

Even those you consider to be your "leaders" can be capable and culpable of inflicting wounds designed to reduce confidence or to set a clear precedent as to where they believe you belong. Sometimes those in leadership struggle with master versus mentor mentality. I remember an experience working for a nonprofit. I assumed that I was being given greater responsibility because I was being trusted by the campus leader because of my work performance measures. I assumed that he was preparing me for future leadership opportunities so I consistently took each task to the next level of performance, to the point of receiving rewards from other department leaders. He asked for a service project, I inspired my team to complete multiple projects. He asked for an update meeting. I prepared a PowerPoint with printouts and the full strategy plan. Whatever the goal my effort was to double or triple it to show my commitment to the cause.

Unfortunately it was not until his comments toward me took a drastic shift that I realized that he was experiencing greater levels of insecurity in comparing his ability with mine.

He would say, "what do you think this is, the Charles show?" or "it is going to be hard for you to repeat that performance. You are the one who set the bar that high."

I realized that his deep insecurity was only growing deeper. I was offered a promotion opportunity by leadership above him without his knowledge. The position did not align with the long-term goals of my family but this manager, having learned of my possible opportunity, did not know that to be the case and began calling me into further questioning.

As he continued the pressure and put me in places where he thought of himself to be the hero, I continued to excel. I had long become aware that his heart's intentions had been corrupted by his lack of belonging but that was not going to keep me from performing to the degree that I felt capable in my area of stewardship. I chose to respectfully decline taking on any new responsibility that would add fuel to the fire and respectfully reminded him that I was only found in places where he himself had put me or leadership. This is why it is important to note on all levels whether those around you believe that they belong. If they do not it is possible that a change in their attitude can occur and cause them to become the rate limiting factor in your life.

If someone around you does not believe that they belong they may encourage you to stop pursuing your determined destination. If you are trying to get yourself in shape and a friend feels that they do not belong they may attempt to sabotage your commitment to your health. Many give up their weight-loss goals after a friend or family member starts working harder to not lose their eating or drinking buddy instead of working to change their life as well.

As you push past the governors you are no longer attached to others by function. You have the right to associate with others based upon freedom. This freedom will cause some people to be forced with the reality of having to change in order to keep up with your new pace and direction. If you have ever tried to embark on a spiritual journey or fully embrace your faith there have likely been friends who immediately felt your change as an indicator that they no longer belonged. No matter how much you love them your new freedom made them feel exposed to how bound they may have been.

Dr. Michael Formica says, "the environment with which we surround ourselves is very often a direct expression of where we are emotionally and psycho-spiritually in our global state of mind." Our identity and circles that we find ourselves in reflect the state of our mind and spirit but also the mind and spirit of those around us. This is why it is ultra-important that not only do you believe that you belong but that your circle also believes the same. When those around us do not believe they belong, their lack of belief can trigger our disbelief and consume energies that would otherwise be best invested in the direction that we need to go. Not only can keeping ourselves in these circles prove damaging to our dreams but they can also prove fatal if we are compelled into nurturing these relationships above our determined destination. In other words our very existence could be threatened by individuals who do not believe they belong and may not want you to recognize that you do.

Dr. Robert Cialdini begins his book *The Psychology of Influence* by telling a true research example of mother turkeys. As mother turkeys have chicks they are wired to listen and respond to a distinct chirp. Should a mother turkey hear this sound it will care for that particular chick. If the chick does not make this sound the turkey will ignore and sometimes kill its own chick.

Researchers continued their investigation using a stuffed replica of a known predator to turkey hatchlings. As expected the mother turkey attacked the stuffed animal viciously upon sight. However when the very same stuffed animal had been implanted with a device that played the distinct chirp the mother turkey accepted it and pulled the animal under its wings. Dr. Cialdini expresses that we too have our own influenceable triggers. Although these triggers are designed to work to our advantage they can be used to manipulate us and redefine our purpose.

I have had the privilege of coaching Yvana to incredible accomplishments. Together we have had the privilege of coaching, training, mentoring and helping many individuals stay the course and push past the governors in their lives. However it is very difficult to remove limiters that are not in our lives but those that are imposed upon us by the limiters in the lives of those within our inner circle who just may in fact, be holding us back even though they desire to see us move forward.

    Sometimes people hold us back because they fear that they will no longer be needed or be an asset. All we can do is invite anyone along for the ride who is truly willing to go but if they cannot hang on then there is no shame in releasing the rip cord for a season until you get where you were trying to go. Sometimes it is worth releasing people who are holding you back as a means of helping them move beyond their comfort zone of living by their limiters. Ironically enough whenever there is a resistance that is released or a weight that is laid aside there is a tremendous slingshot effect that can take place. That is what we call the slingshot effect and it can maximize your propulsion like never before.

FLICKER OF FIRED (FORTITUDE)

Having a sincere belief that you belong will give you courage and confidence when potential problems threaten that conviction. Trust us, you will need both courage and confidence. Potential can almost feel as though it invites or incites moments of great complexity and perplexity. If you are not aware of this potential problem you run the risk of spiraling out of control or off the prepared path made for you. There will be moments that your faith will be tested on account of the very words that fuel the belief that you belong. There are countless examples of individuals with so much potential who threw it all away because they could not remain focused on where they were headed and gave up.

THE FLIGHT OF YOUR LIFE

We have discussed the significance of passion, repentance, self-discipline, force, potential, velocity and even propulsion. Yet one thing remains that sets those who will experience the flight of their life from those who will not. *Fortitude.* Having the audacity to want more for your life and to expect more for and from others is a direct challenge to the status quo. It is in opposition to the way things are, the way things have always been and the way it has been done. That may make other people uncomfortable and resistant to your propulsive efforts. Even those closest to you may feel that your potential is a problem because it does not fit into the picture of possibility for them.

This potential-problem can cause very hurtful experiences and may even make you question your efforts and direction despite having already committed to the work and having made every effort to put yourself in propulsive positioning. Employers may even shift their attitude without regard for your expressed desires to improve areas of your responsibility. You taking a propulsive position may be grounds enough for an employer to push you out of your role or out the door. You must ask yourself if you have the absolute conviction that what you are doing is right for your company, your team, your family and ultimately, yourself. Then you must decide whether you would stick to those convictions when they are challenged or even threatened.

This is a real potential problem. It may mean having your job threatened. It could mean being denied advancement opportunity because you advocate for it. It could mean being forced to resign not because you are underperforming but because of overperformance because of actually being a good employee. Instead of reducing your fire to a flicker as expected your flame creates a hot seat under your boss that makes it difficult to justify their position. You may be threatened with termination being fired as your

POTENTIAL AND PROBLEMS

performance outshines those who cannot contain you. This is a real occurrence in the workforce. Bad bosses compel good employees to leave. There may genuinely be nothing wrong with you but the problems you may face or are facing could be because of your potential.

You do not seek the forefront or the limelight and yet you cannot seem to avoid it. Despite your best effort to remain unseen you are always being seen. Despite your best efforts to keep your head down and hidden behind the scenes your work calls you to the front and the results point right back to you. You are like a city on a hill. No matter how hard you try a city on a hill cannot be hidden. No matter where you go or who you work with there is no way around this. Whatever the job or function you always take it to the top. This causes unnecessary friction for you no matter how hard you try. As you maximize your potential your presence may awaken those around you to the full possibility of their potential. You will experience increases in those who desire to work with you. Volunteers may serve with you willingly and clients would rather deal with you. You may see now how this could become a potential problem.

It took us years to comprehend this potential problem. We tried to fit into the boxes but no matter how hard we tried, the box would explode. We told ourselves that if we continued to perform beyond the levels of expectations more freedom and opportunity would be extended. So we pushed the performance envelope even further. All we found was that we were being tested repeatedly and it seemed as though the harder we worked, the more we produced and the faster we were being pushed out of a job. We were led to believe that the greatest sign of leadership is to work oneself out of a job. We had now worked ourselves out of three and in all three we had no disciplinary issues, no rumors of misconduct, no record of missing the mark or dropping

THE FLIGHT OF YOUR LIFE

the ball and no unjust or unjustified encounters. The only similarity—the person above us felt that we were after their position and felt that we were disrupting the status quo they had become comfortable with.

We did not curse, raise our voice, or step out of character and we always left with gifts, handshakes and hugs. We would leave our post with grace, dignity and humility even when our removal was unethical or on the verge of being illegal. When news of our resignation reached our colleagues we would often be thrown a party with cake, cards, letters and love in thanks for our service. The contrast juxtaposition we were enduring internally was astounding. We were secretly asked to resign by a singular party then publicly heralded and honored by those we served with and those who served under our leadership. It was allegorically raining on one side of the street and bright sunshine on the other.

We were two of the only people that we knew who had been removed from positions because we were "too good" or "possessed too many talents." That did not make sense to us. We did not have the awakening moment until our thirties that our pain was partnering with our purpose. Purpose is not and will not be relegated to any position. It requires a lot of spiritual work, reflection and discernment to wrap your mind around the fact that your potential can actually be your problem. This is difficult to endure because it is the fire within you that is being used to test you. As you may discover as you begin to express the power of your potential and things begin to propel forward, the tighter the line becomes. You can give up or the line must give way. Those ultimately are the only options.

Here we were unemployed with master's degrees and leadership and management experience that would take tens of years for others to acquire. We had a small business

POTENTIAL AND PROBLEMS

but we had not yet invested all that we could have into getting it off the ground. We were shiny and bright when we first took our positions and now we were leaving with scratches and damage by people we trusted to propel us to our next level and there it was—the potential problem. We had trusted other people with the process of our propulsion. We had believed their promises and put ourselves in their hands and were patronized. Damn, how could we have missed that? How could you miss that? Easily. When you are not motivated by ulterior motives you assume that the people you encounter are genuinely good and do not have ulterior motives either.

I will never forget one day I was wrestling through how Yvana and I could have been wronged so greatly and spitefully. As I stood in front of my bathroom mirror looking right into my eyes, I distinctly heard the voice of God speaking these words: "you understand why I have allowed you to keep going through this the last few years. You believed that man has your best interest at heart. They can never have your best interest at heart. Only I have your best interest at heart. They do not know it and they do not own it."

It later occurred to me a few years back a stranger spoke to me with a word of encouragement. He said, "guard your heart with all diligence. Do not trust this heart to just anyone. This heart is precious and there will be many who will want to damage it."

I did not recognize that he was speaking concerning an area of my greatest testing our greatest testing. Now after looking back, I completely understand. The flame within both of our hearts has always been more than a flicker yet despite our impact and results, here we were being forced to resign or get fired. We were being tested and had not yet learned the lesson. Each test was trying to help us see that we were made for more. We were being refined by the very fire within us.

    This is a blessing not a curse. The power of our propulsion is best expressed in repeatability. We were being fitted with endurance with each test. We were being fortified with *fortitude*. Fortitude is the courage in pain or adversity. It is bravery, strength of mind, strength of character, moral strength, toughness of spirit and firmness of purpose. It only comes by the testing of our faith. We had no clue that each test was a gauge that was being used to see just how persevering we were. Did we have grit? Was who we thought we were an idea in our minds or a truth in our Spirit? Were we going to give up, cave in, fight to hold on or trust that we were being given our direction that sets us in motion and cannot be stopped? With each test we realized that we were getting stronger that our skills were increasing, that our hunger for growth was increasing and we knew that we were truly unstoppable. We realized that we were only going to be held to the limit that we allow or accept.

    Until you develop the necessary fortitude purpose will not propel you forward. You will continue to be challenged with lack of clarity and vision until you stand firm in the testing. You may find yourself in and out of "jobs" until you recognize purpose is doing its job developing you within each one of them. You will be put into the fire over and over again until you embrace it, become it. Be content with it. Then you will be equipped for the good work prepared for you. You will neither be compelled when you are low or high in need or in a season of prosperity. You will be able to do all things. Instead of being controlled by whether you will have a job or not you will remain in control recognizing that all that you need is within you.

    Your identity is not in your work; it is in your *worth*. Your tests are not insults they are assessments of your greatest *attribute*. Fortitude determines your self-worth. There is nothing wrong with you. You were created with purpose on purpose. You are neither trash nor worthless despite how many times you have been misled to believe so. Someone who was entrusted with you does not mean that they were not intimidated by the bigness of you. You may have been removed or released because your potential was beyond comprehension.

The potential problem you may endure serves a dual purpose. Your fortitude could expose or reveal inefficiencies and deficiencies of those who have been entrusted with your operation. It is frustrating to know your potential then be placed under the responsibility of someone who is not willing to invest the time to learn how you operate or function. The more rejection you face the more you may be compelled to feel undervalued and underestimated.

In the film *Real Steel* Hugh Jackman invests in a new fighting robot from Japan with all of the upgrades, bells and whistles. The model is unlike anything he has ever experienced before. Immediately upon opening the contents he is amazed with the advanced technology and begins shouting commands before spending any time with it. Instead of learning how it operates and making adjustments to allow the robot to function as designed he tries to force it to be exactly as he envisioned instead of its design. Despite his commands the robot does nothing. The robot is visibly attentive, as indicated by the head movements, but does not function. Just as quickly as he had been excited to have the robot his frustration reaches a peak and he labels the robot defective despite its potential. Then his son, in the humble voice of a child, begins to give direction to the robot in the language encoded by the designer and the machine displays its power without hesitation or reservation. The issue was neither the design or the designer, it was the operator.

THE FLIGHT OF YOUR LIFE

You are not a robot however. If you are enduring the pain so get something out of it. See the way that you deserve to be treated, compensated, directed, trained and utilized and to function and produce. Recall these are assets. It is often not until we encounter this potential problem that we begin to see our self-worth. Stand fast during the testing. The time is short and the pressure is building. You are on the verge of taking the flight of your life. Whether you are sent back to the designer or to another operator you will understand that it is all a part of the perfect work. Rest in the faith that comes with believing that you belong. Allow the testing of that faith to produce fortitude which will keep you from giving up. Once fortitude is developed you will be stronger than ever, complete and lacking nothing for your journey.

> Your identity is not in your work;
> it is in your *worth*.

FIGHT AND FLIGHT (FOCUS)

One of the more common potential problems you may face is keeping your focus forward in the presence of distraction. We are not necessarily discussing all of the external distractions we mentioned in earlier chapters. We can easily become distracted by shifts in attitudes regarding our potential and progress. You may like to think that everyone is genuinely excited for your decision to maximize your potential (physical, mental, athletic or career) as you take new ground and enter new air space but this is never true. There will be individuals who disapprove of you simply *because* of your potential and in some cases your pigmentation—but we digress. Who you are, where you are headed may not always serve as inspiration but rather insult to those who may be watching. You must develop a sense of focus that keeps you

POTENTIAL AND PROBLEMS

from being moved by either even when the shifts in attitude lead to attempts to discredit or undervalue your potential.

This potential problem is based upon our desire to feel accepted or understood. You may even feel compelled to turn back when you observe how unsettled others are with your determined direction. If you have spent the time preparing, learning new skills and challenging your own biases and fears you are not going to be satisfied with the box that you may have been in. Your persistent propulsion challenges your fit within the well-defined boundaries of the status quo. Despite holding a clear line of sight we can slowly begin to shift our attitude based upon those who continue to cross our eye line. This loss of focus can cause us to relinquish our purpose for fear of other people. When we do this we are left with one of two options—we either run from it or self-destruct.

You may have heard of *fight or flight*. This complex is an involuntary or instinctive nervous system response to any perceived stress, attack or potentially harmful event. This response readies us to either *resist* the threat or *run* from it. Either way we may lose focus and find ourselves engaged in an altercation designed to take us off our path or running and forsaking the payment of progress. Our natural response is not always the best response and requires great focus. There are moments in life where being prepared for a fight is warranted. However this is the difference between being prepared and unprepared. One is centered by the focus of having a prepared strategy of maneuvers that can influence the outcome of the circumstance while minimizing or eliminating the risk of destruction. The art of flight *is* to fight.

The fundamentals of competitive sport are based upon managing these variables and maintaining a focus on moving an object or self forward. Records are broken, goals are made and points are scored by moving forward. In competition with opposing sides the ability to use flight as an offensive advantage can dictate who moves forward and ultimately, who will leave in victory. Championship-level athletes train hours upon hours to learn how to use their speed and power to propel their team forward. The quicker of the group is intentionally used to shift and maneuver to avoid having forward momentum cease. Flight is found in almost every sport and the entire game is determined by it. Flight *is* the focus. Flight *is* the fight.

There may come peers who are appalled by your audacity to advance. Keep flying. They may be coworkers who feel that you do not deserve advancement. Keep flying. There may be someone who becomes jealous enough to make their disdain very clear. Keep flying. Some people may pull away while some will press toward you with the hope of attaching themselves to your progress. Keep flying. You may be let go from your job, team or position because of your attempt to increase your potential. Keep flying. Flight is the focus. Flight is the fight. The more you focus on remaining in flight the better you become at shifting your attitude in response to the environment and those in them. Maneuverability is the product of focus and experience.

You are already daring to defy the odds and the expectations of you that do not line up with your expectations of yourself. You are more aware of your own attitude and needed adjustments. As you encounter adversity now you can trust yourself to make adjustments and decisions more quickly that have a greater purpose in maintaining your propulsion. Using flight as your fight will allow you to keep focus on your horizon even when it is not in sight.

As you enter new air space and someone comes in a bit too close for comfort adjust quickly. When a person attempts to blindside you in an attempt to compel you to engage them on their terms, do not indulge. Trust your instincts

POTENTIAL AND PROBLEMS

quickly shift your attitude, keep composure and keep flying. You are taking ground as long as you do not turn back. Win every second that you remain in flight. Your refusal to make their shift in attitude your focus only frustrates theirs. As long as you refuse to turn over your possession you remain on offense even when it appears that you are on defense. Remain focused on the bigger picture, the flight of your life. This will keep you from lying down or dumbing down your potential as you continue to maximize your potential.

By now you may be putting together the pieces of what we may be alluding to. Taking your potential to the next level of propulsion is not always a comfortable or easy ride. You must remain steadfast, aware and vigilant as a challenge can arise at any moment. The flight of your life will be a dogfight. A dogfight is a war phrase typically describing airborne combat. You may have seen footage or film depicting the intensity and high-stakes maneuverability required to keep a pilot in flight. As long as they are in flight they are winning in the fight to stay aloft.

Skilled pilots use banks, rolls, splits, yo-yos and scissors to ensure survival. These maneuvers require focus. Even when projectiles are being fired at them remaining focused on flight allows them to handle the pressure. What you are trying to accomplish will put you into immense pressure. Pressure is the privilege of propulsion. Great amounts of pressure can be created on the inside of you to resist that which you encounter on the outside. Great amounts of pressure, or g-force, is experienced with greater levels of acceleration. Great criticism and challenge comes with great composure. If your potential is of no concern there would be no pressure because of your potential. There would be no potential problems to face. Your pressure is a privilege. Keep flying.

THE FLIGHT OF YOUR LIFE

There may come a time in your business where a competitor sets a roadblock in the path of your propulsion. Do not stop moving. Even if the obstruction requires that you turn on a dime make the decision with confidence. Trust that you have what it takes to withstand the pressure, make the necessary adjustment and *pivot* and propel even harder. There may come a time when you must make an adjustment based upon the perceived adjustments being made to corner you and force you to comply with a direction that is not in the best interest of your determined destination. Keeping your focus will set up an appropriately timed *feint*. A feint is an aggressive maneuver that gives the indication of one direction while setting up another rapid maneuver that confuses the opposition and uses their momentum to your favor.

The more you focus on self-awareness, self-respect and self-care the more in control you will feel. You may be labeled self-seeking, self-ambitious, selfish and another iteration of your true self by those who will eventually realize that they cannot master by outmaneuvering you. When you begin hearing of private attacks on your character do not seek to defend yourself. Keep flying. Let your work and worth speak for you. As you remain focused on forward you will accelerate with even greater momentum and find yourself in another class. This is where the final test is and it will be cumulative. It will test your will for freedom, your faith and friendships. It will absolutely test your fortitude and your focus. As you begin flying with skill, earning and commanding the airspace, you will find yourself in new company. Suddenly feelings of unworthiness and lack of belonging may compel you to take it down a notch and to fly a bit lower than your potential has made room for.

Do not slow down and do not turn over your authority. You have already been given permission for propulsion. You

POTENTIAL AND PROBLEMS

have one job—that is to absolutely stay composed. Do not feel compelled to slow down or stop once you feel confident that it is time to take flight. Now that you have become acquainted with potential, power, propulsion and the problems that may arise on account of your potential, you are cleared to take flight. There are a few things we want to remember:

1. The only permission you need is your own.
2. You should always push limits and limiters.
3. Pick a point of interest and stop at nothing until you get there.
4. Propel others with your accomplishments and innovation.

Your pressure is a privilege.
Keep flying.

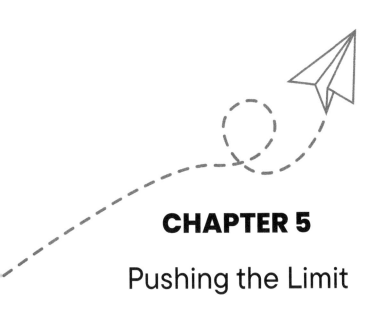

CHAPTER 5

Pushing the Limit

Have you ever pushed a vehicle to its limit and noticed that it was well beneath the maximum speed presented on the dashboard? Despite pressing your foot through the floorboard the vehicle was not moving any faster. This is because the vehicle was under the control or influence of a *limiter*. We mentioned limiters a few moments ago but we want to discuss them as they do not necessarily prevent propulsion. But they do limit potential. Limiters are instruments of limitation that have been wired or coded into the *control units* or brains of a vehicle. They are designed to limit speed, output or any additional degrees of freedom to cap performance to submaximal levels.

Yvana and I once had an experience with a moving truck that limited our speed to seventy miles per hour. I recall trying to press the accelerator in a double-pump fashion hoping that the vehicle would experience a speed burst as the cars in some of our favorite arcade games would. No matter how hard I pressed that truck was not going above seventy unless we were going downhill! Even then I would jerk my body forward to see if I could get just a little more performance beyond the limiter. Limiters typically work in one of two ways: they limit the flow of air or fuel. You may already be drawing a correlation here between life and the function of limiters. Limiters are given authority to reduce or "manage" *flow* or creative freedom or limit available resources to give potential its boundaries. Flow is the process in which tasks in a business take place.

The idea of limiters is not necessarily ill-intended. There are other discussions to be had when it comes to the literal application. For instance limiters can be safety mechanisms put in place to reduce the risk of overuse or overreaching. However in the flight of life, limiters can become the tool of choice used to keep any particular person from overachieving. This is the difference between artistically managing process versus managing people. Great managers manage processes and mentor or *administer* to the people. If a person with great potential cannot be handled or does not conform a limited manager can become a limiter who deems any person they cannot bend to their will as unteachable. Allow us a minute on this subject before moving on.

Some of the most impressive individuals and team leaders find themselves released because they are designed to push their team, culture and processes forward. If this has happened to you this is typically a greater reflection of management than you as an employee. There is an art to and significance of having properly trained, emotionally intelligent managers who do not seek control but seek and understand the community. Entrusting individuals who are capable of celebrating and utilizing the strengths of those whose potential pushes productivity and the status quo is the lifeblood of innovation. It is one thing to work with a challenging individual within a system and another to work with an individual who challenges the system with their work.

Managers whose approach is limitation as their means of leadership exposes their need for comfort or control and their motives should be questioned as to whether they truly want to move the company and others forward.

There are no universal industry standards that dictate how limiters may impact performance. This supports subjective applications of classification or control that are based upon preference rather than potential, progress or production. If you are being honest you may be the limiter in your organization, family or team that has been holding others back from expressing the fullness of their potential. If so recognize it, admit it and take a bold new direction. Do not go into the office trying to be something you are not but be all that you can be in this moment until it becomes who you are.

Limiters may not always be easy to recognize. One way to observe the limiters or limits that you have put in place is to assess your circle and structure—not your personal circle but that of those you are in a position to serve. If you are a manager or CEO what does your room look like? Does everyone reflect you, your ideas and ideals? Are they all versions of yourself with minor modifications? Does everyone agree with you? If you are an employee ask the same questions. Are you represented in the room? Are you allowed to disagree and offer alternative solutions? Are you empowered and encouraged to try bold ideas and stretch your imagination? Are you given the resources that you need to enjoy your work and succeed? Are you encouraged to pursue opportunities for advancement?

Questions like these will help you identify limiters that you may have set up or that you may be expected to perform under. In either case, you may be burning out or creating burnout. Compelling individuals or being compelled to limit who you are in order to fit the constructs of comfort will always create internal conflict. As we explore this next chapter our hope is that you become more sensitive to what or who may be actively limiting your flow or restricting the resources and energy that you would use to maximize propulsion. We intend for this opportunity to give you the courage to recognize individuals whom you may be intended to serve but might be limiting. Accept the challenge to look at your relationships and how you relate to *your* ship. Whether you are a team captain, a CEO, an entrepreneur, educator, student, spouse or parent none of that matters.

Limiters do not always have to be a person who is hierarchically above you. It could be a vice that slows down your progress or keeps you from expressing your full potential. Do not overlook or dismiss the impact that the ego, addiction, perverse materials and encounters can have after being encoded into your soul. These things can create debilitating limiters to both flow and resources and can be the hardest to recognize. They can also be the most stubborn to be removed because they are bolted through our exterior into the root of our inner being: our minds, will, emotions. These limiters are called *soul ties* which are bound to our past and limit us is in our present.

Soul ties and vices are not a matter of legality. We are not here to make you feel judged *but* we would be careless if we did not remind you of why you are reading this book in the first place and that *you* have the seat of power, authority and judgment to condemn or release whatever limiter presents itself in *your* life. Just because you do something does not mean that you enjoy it enough to stay forever bound to it. That is your choice but we are not here to commend or correct your choices. You are.

Remember that all things are permissible but not all things are beneficial. We can all agree that recreational drugs and alcohol do limit our senses, limit or impair judgment and limit our connection to reality. So if it is a limiter you must decide whether it is worthy of the potential consequences. In the same manner your limiter may be unhealthy eating habits that limit your flow of health, limit your self-esteem and self-confidence or limit your resource of time. Your limiter could be money and material possessions. You may have a lot of both but your lifestyle is above your means and you are actually keeping less than someone who makes less. Whatever your limiter you are the only person who has the right to decide whether it will remain or be challenged.

Limiters can keep us from making moves toward changing our course at the exact moment that we need change most. In order to push beyond them you must decide that you are willing to push so hard that the limiter must malfunction or short-circuit. Take the time to learn and observe your circuitry. You may need to label your limiters and what they limit so as to not damage any attached components. This is another piece of taking *ownership*. We have such a strong zeal for this word. It is something that most of us do not naturally do. We are all easily capable of placing blame or responsibility on what is done to us but we fail to recognize that it was we ourselves who chose to accept their burden as our own. What does not belong to you does not belong to you. What does, does. Taking ownership is like having the certificate title of owning a vehicle. If you own it you can modify it, but if you are making payments then you do not own it.

If you want to go faster and go further you can only accept ownership of your potential and purpose. Stop choosing to lease life. Do whatever you have to do in order to get those papers. Declare your stance with the receipts that show your potential belongs to you. Then it will be up to you to decide which modifications you need to make in order to maximize propulsion. You were not

> Stop choosing to lease life.

born with limiters. You were born limitless. You did not know what sin was, you did not know what disappointment was or crime, bias, hatred or any other limiter. You were coming to sense with being alive at all.

If you do not put in the work or take ownership, you will always remain at a certain level in your career, relationships and destiny. Your experiences, encounters, actions and emotions create impulses for potential that increase in strength until they become locked in like *muscle memory*. In like manner if you choose to make excuses here or to leave the authority in the control of your limiters the impulse will become so normal that it will become your existence. Your potential will always express itself and will reflect your limiter if you are not careful becoming the dysfunction in which you operate.

In some cases limiters that remain can be overridden or disabled until they are removed. You have always had the key and authority to deny access, change habits, mindsets, emotions and responses. Whenever limiters give an order you can pause and override the order. This may be a simple step that you can make in your life. When a limiter compels you to do one thing you say out loud, "*override.*" And choose to do what will bring about the best propulsive outcome. You do not have to live in a perpetual state of impeded progress. You have to decide, *this is not how I want this life to continue to go.* Repent choose to turn back toward where you should be going and commit to living that way even if it hurts. Repentance is the foundation for reestablishing ownership.

Repentance is more than sorrow for things that you have done. It is also letting go of limiting things done to you so that you can leave them where they are. Your job is to get limiters out and off of you as quickly as possible because they intend to impede you from getting where you intend to go. Stop waiting for your turn if you have been missing the one you should have taken. Continue to put in the work, make sacrifices, serve faithfully but do not give your authority over to limiters.

If you have been repeatedly overlooked for that position or promotion;

If you have been held in a role or function despite being the best candidate for another opportunity or advancement;

If you have genuinely invested yourself in keeping the right relationships and healthy boundaries and offering your honor and respect but still feel unseen or undervalued;

If your team, culture or company has not advanced people like you and does not reflect the core values that you have worked hard to honor and embody;

If you have done all that you can and have completed all that you were expected to do, then give the same energy and intensity toward all that you expect of you take back your authority and remove the limiter lenses. You may actually realize that your limiter was only in your mind. Do not be like the elephant who has been held captive with a rope around its ankle when it could rip the rope right off of the stake.

Take ownership then take action. Do not get angry, just get active. Get your mind and emotions out of the gutter and get back to the goals that God has given you. Stop being so concerned with what someone else will think. That is false humility, false honor and idolatry. Taking ownership is your highest form of honor. You have the gift of direction and it has been given by God. So go for it. You may not even have to leave your current role or function to make movement happen. Your current role or function may serve as the inspiration and competitive edge you will need to differentiate yourself. You may have had an idea and tried to present it to your leadership and they rejected it. That does not mean it was a bad idea. It means that the idea was given to you for a reason. If you do it and it works be glad. You have found a niche that you can fill and economically speaking, the riches are in the niches.

There should be no hard feelings in your seeking advancement, especially when you are repeatedly denied an opportunity to do so. If your seeking advancement was intended to advance those around you and the company, team, family or function you are committed to and they do not see it, then do not scrap the entire idea. Make it work. This is not entitlement but empowerment. Move your faith. Move your feet. Move yourself forward. Whatever needs to change will only change when you commit to change.

Removing limiters in your life is sometimes as easy as moving away from the limiter. Up until this point we have talked about removing limiters but you also have the option of removing yourself from limiters and limiting environments. You can remove yourself from limiting conversations. If the people around you are not talking about moving themselves or others forward then you move yourself out of that conversation. Once you decide to no longer give limiters any authority in your life or in areas that do not pertain to a particular role or function, you will begin to see how your potential has always been a resource.

Here are some ways that can actively remove limiters in your life and put yourself in a propulsive position. The first is *network*. Relationships have the greatest impact on realization. There is a saying, "*your network is your net worth.*" If you are in a role that does not challenge you or does not allow you to challenge your abilities make connections with other industry professionals or teams. Join a networking group in your area. Participate in a small group or a mastermind. If you have kids you are already part of a networking group, especially if your child or children are in any extracurricular activities. Get to know other parents. If you are in college join intramural sports, student government, a club, fraternity or sorority. Choose to pursue these relationships looking to improve your life, not just social status.

Second *add value*. Do not assume that people should want to have you around or that they need you around. Make it clear what you hope to get out of a relationship and be plain about what you want to *give* to the other person. Yvana and I genuinely believe in this. We ask people what they would like to get out of a relationship with us up front and we also ask and establish that we are seeking a relationship with the intent to give.

> Removing limiters in your life is sometimes as easy as moving away from the limiter.

"What can I bring to this relationship that will add value to your life? How can I help you and where you are trying to go?" Ask people this question and watch how quickly you start being trusted with friendship or connections. This has allowed us to form genuine relationships with professionals across industry and sports all because we are sincere about creating meaningful connections and seeing how we may be of service first. Do not skip over that last point. The levels that your potential is made for can also be limited by intentions and ulterior motives. We will cover this concept at a later point.

Third *present progress*. If your words do not match your action or follow-through then you have lost momentum before you have begun. People are less willing to invest in you if you are not willing to invest in yourself. Do not just follow through on your word but follow through on your words concerning yourself. You should be able to present progress in areas and not always your limits. Even if you are making very little progress that progress will inspire others to assist you. That speaks volumes of your value and what you value. There have been so many stories of people who have seen us dedicating to making progress who have given their services and made a phone call or an introduction on our behalf because we presented progress. We are not living by what limits us, we are actively working out of our liberty. Apply this concept to other areas of your life. If you are serious about changing lives for the better do not talk about it, be about it. If you are serious about losing weight do not talk about it, be about it. If you are serious about earning a spot on someone's team or roster do not just talk about it, be about it.

By investing in your own health and well-being people will hold your perspective with more gravitas. Maybe your limiter is a health condition. We understand, but you can still apply these steps. Connecting with health and wellness professionals, trainers, coaches or therapists can present relationships that can literally add value to your life. You can add value to their lives by taking their advice and recommendations seriously and referring others to their services. If your process is too complex to complete alone, take ownership that you may be your own limiter. As we have made abundantly clear there is no shame in seeking professional help or instruction as long as you are determined to remove any stubborn limiters in your life.

As you become more passionate about ownership you will become more in tune with the status of who you are. Take your seat. That is what we are inspiring you to do—to see yourself as the only person made to sit in the seat of determining your destination. You may be an employee at a particular firm or business but you are always going to be the CEO of yourself. Each one of us has been given all that pertains to life and the gift of direction within ourselves. As we continue we hope that we have inspired you to remove the blinders and to see beyond the walls of your confinement or labor. There is a world of opportunity and relationships; there are opportunities available that will maximize your potential. Boss up and take ownership.

BE THE BOSS

Renowned motivational and educational speaker Anthony O'Neal tells his story of a conversation between him and a friend. I have had the privilege and honor of serving as an emcee for him during my time in vocational ministry and have heard him tell quite a few stories but this one in particular breathes life into our last topic of discussion and how to use it to push the limit of what we cannot control. Anthony took a few matters or issues of concern to him that were outside of his control. Thinking he would receive sympathy or empathy for that matter, what he ended up receiving was a life lesson. He received a wake-up call that would propel him to take ownership of what he could control and remove the limits of that which he could not. The advice was simple: *mind your business.*

    Caught off guard by the response Anthony responded, "what do you mean? I am minding my business!" As the conversation proceeds Anthony becomes enlightened by the power of what had been given to him. The insight: "your mind is your business." Did you catch that? *Your mind is your business!* As the newly reintroduced CEO of *you* it is your job to manage your own mind. It is your job to curate what you intake. It is your job to evaluate and to implement. It is up to you to partner with the gift of direction in you to set the *strategic processes* and *partnerships* that will move *you*. Your vision, mission, objectives and decisions should be in

THE FLIGHT OF YOUR LIFE

line with *the goal* and should always drive you and others to it. We will discuss these things soon but for now, let us continue to discuss your role as the CEO of *you*.

Limits and limiters in the workforce are put in place and evaluated on how well they are at enforcing the limitations while managing the freedoms of function. As we touched upon in the chapter introduction, limiters are distinctly empowered to manage intellectual, influential and inspirational capacities of each employee with the bottom line in mind. It is important that you comprehend that is their purpose. This is their role. They are not your enemy no matter how much of one they present themselves to be. They are not your roadblock. Even though they may intentionally make every effort to limit the full expression of your gifts, talents and abilities, they are serving their purpose and may even be doing so expertly and professionally. No matter the relationship or current challenge you must still take ownership of where you want to go and why.

Keep your mind on your business. Your mind is your business. Even if you are currently under supervision that intentionally limits your capabilities or progress *mind your business*. Even if there is a strategic process designed to keep you exactly where you are, as CEO of *you*, have a plan for yourself commit to it and know that *the goal* is propelling you forward. You cannot control your boss, your coach or anyone else in positional authority but you can remain in control of spiritual authority. This authority is the one that your life will be waged on. It is also the authority that war will be waged upon as you seek to remove or push your limits.

There are a few things that you can begin to mind immediately that will guide you as you navigate through the tight spaces intended to limit your propulsion. First you must take ownership of your personal brand and statement of purpose. By doing so you will preserve your *competitive advantage*, which will give you confidence to let your actions elevate your reputation and which will be important as you begin to put yourself in a propulsive position. Your competitive advantage is a result of (1) evaluating your potential and preparing for potential problems by assessing your strengths, weaknesses, opportunities and threats; (2) clearly defining your aspirations by clarifying *the ultimate goal* and; (3) setting your personal performance targets while observing key performance indicators and setting benchmarks or points of interest along the way.

As you embrace these concepts you will see an increased productivity and the gift of direction within you will inspire you to keep yourself in a propulsive position at all times. This will become something that makes you uniquely different. It will help guide your decisions on where to invest your resources and relationships. By having this insight you will keep costs low, mitigate risk and have a clear vision for the future. It is okay if you currently feel stuck in the middle. The term *stuck in the middle* is actually a business term used to describe businesses that have too many conflicting strategies and directions. At least you are at the crossroads, the tipping point. Even if you feel exhausted and overwhelmed having pursued multiple strategies trying to get to the next level you are on the verge of streamlining your operational costs and putting more energy that will maximize the profitability of your life.

> Keep your mind on your business. Your mind is your business.

Much like a restaurant with a thousand items on the menu you will find degrees of freedom as you begin cutting away or outsourcing things that are good but may not be bringing a return worthy of investing your energies in that direction at this time. Some things may even serve you better if they are *outsourced* or given to someone else to do at a lower opportunity cost while still contributing to your desired performance outcomes. Hopefully you are seeing the connection between propulsive power and removing limits by minding your business. As you begin to see yourself as a business your vision and scope becomes bigger. Instead of seeing yourself in relation to your current job, role or position on the team you begin to see yourself as something beyond that limitation—the same way many athletes have evolved beyond the sport into business and, in some cases, ownership of their own team or franchise. Taking ownership and embracing the gift of direction within you will focus your mind on remaining in a propulsive position no matter your current position.

Defining your mission, aspirations and goals and then taking action based upon these will streamline your resources and will keep you from saying *yes* to anything that does not align with *the goal* or your determined destination. This practice will also empower you to *say no* to things that do not propel you toward either. The word *no* will also keep you humble and allow you the time needed to evaluate and to learn so that your response may eventually be yes. The word *no* is your greatest yes. As you continue to embrace ownership and begin to renew your mind and to see it as your business, your established no will mean yes to areas that will increase your propulsive power.

Learning to say no is one of the most liberating powers you will develop as you hone your focus by mitigating the potential problems that can occur due to emotion. Emotional decision making is often the pitfall for the secure CEO. Emotions are helpful tools but if not balanced with clear and cut statements of purpose emotions can be manipulated, motivated or compelled to move away from what will propel your life and the life of others further along. As an added bonus taking ownership and renewing your mind serves as a type of rebirth. You will begin to k(no)w yourself and see more clearly what you are truly capable of.

"NO" YOUR WORTH

Your greatest *know* is your *no*. *The ability to* say no will increase your worth and add value to your power and purpose. No your worth. This revelation has the power to propel you beyond settling for positions that only fit your abilities and not your destiny. This revelation has the power to propel you far above superficial relationships that only serve temporary pleasures into a thriving, satisfying, healthy, fulfilling love relationship with a committed life partner. This revelation has the power to propel you beyond the stereotypes, misjudgments, convictions, traps, pitfalls and your own propensities to failure by reconnecting you with the gift of direction in you. It matters not what your name may be perceived as today, you can take it back. You have the power to remove the limiters by taking ownership today and giving it new meaning by tomorrow.

Your greatest *know* is your *no*.

No matter how far from your name you may have ventured all it takes is that audacious turn toward what you know in your heart that it should mean. Even if you are inspired to clarify what you no longer want your name associated with or perceived as and limited to you can begin saying no to those things and yes to anything that propels you in the direction of what it could be. A simple exercise that can help you establish how you see yourself is to come up with a personal slogan. In business this is called a *positioning statement*. These statements summarize worth and clarify the significance of a name. It creates vision by communicating value, attitudes and propositions of value. If others have used a positioning statement to declare your potential, offering or your entire life as worthless, know today that you have the power to say no to them.

Some slogans you may have heard regarding your life could be:

> "Never going to be enough."
>
> "A deadbeat dad."
>
> "Divorced with two kids."
>
> "Stubborn like your mother."

If you recall our discussion on rehearsal you may have a few of these phrases that you repeat to yourself over and over. As you hear them or repeat them they become what you say yes to and increase your potential for actions that determine your worth. Take a moment to write a list of positioning statements that were meant to declare your worth that you do not agree with. Draw or imagine yourself writing the word *no* over them. On another sheet of paper or maybe in your mind write your own statements that declare your worth. Try to keep them under six or fewer words. Make sure these statements describe the real you, who you really are, and who you want people to see.

A name is a word or set of words by which a person, brand or thing is known, addressed or referred to. Names have value. They have worth. They can contain a plethora of emotions and years of history in as little as two letters. Names can even communicate the hopes, dreams and destiny of an individual. In one name or a few that have been stringed together there could be an identifier that can paint a picture of power that shapes perception or influences how we perceive value. If you want to give yourself a bit of courage it may be of some interest to you to investigate the deeper meaning of your own name. You may find that your name has hidden gems that were left as a clue to give your life meaning to let you know how much you are worth. You may be surprised. No matter how it was given to you there are always hidden messages within our names that indicate what we were made for. It may even give you the power to eliminate anything that does not allow you to live up to or add value to your name. There is more to your name than you might know. It contains your power to say no.

Names often offer clues into personality or *personal-reality*. Your personal-reality is how you see yourself in relation to the world and how you imagine that the world sees you. Your name may reveal a reflection of characteristics that once belonged to another bearer of the name in the family before you. Even if your name is atypical or unconventional, the very nature of your name was intended for you to stand out in a crowd. That in itself, offers insight into the purposes that you may fulfill given your bold, artistic or adventurous name. Names give power to messages. Once a name is spoken the intention will never be returned. As we discussed in the beginning of the book, your name is associated with calling. Calling is associated with passion. Passion is associated with potential. Potential is associated with power, power with purpose. Like the ripples of water, sound waves have been reverberating through your very existence before the moment you were born. Remember, God who knew your name before anyone who would hear it passed your name on to you. Your name just like your life, may have come through your parents but *the goal* was given

THE FLIGHT OF YOUR LIFE

to you before your first breath and is dedicated to propel you toward all of the greatness that began in you.

> There is more to your name than you might know. It contains your power to say no.

    To make this point a bit more relative, let us take a look at Charles's name. This may help you as you put in the work to k(no)w yourself and better align that knowledge of self with the responsibility of ownership and possessing the power of *the goal*. Charles is believed to come from the Germanic word *Karl*. This word most appropriately means "free man." The name Bailey comes from the English surname *bailiff*. A bailiff as you may be familiar, was known as chief officer to as many as one hundred officials serving the highest courts of the king. This is where the term *a king's man* or *kingsman* comes from. Charles reflects these perceived qualities genuinely and authentically, and his characteristics fit this name. Ironically Charles is also a junior. The similarities between him and his father are undeniable. What is more interesting is that Charles has not seen his father since he was five years old, yet Charles recognizes his father in himself often.

    Charles is a creative free-spirited man with a strong regal presence and a bent toward social justice, equality and advocacy. He is passionate and outspoken about his faith, spiritual authority and conviction of Christ. He believes that all life, but his in particular, serves a greater purpose to move culture forward and liberate souls to the honor of his King. Charles does not function well in micromanaging environments and is incredibly self-sufficient. He has a unique ability to create great spheres of influence. He can quickly gather, train and release others into delegated responsibilities and point them toward purpose with foresight and enthusiasm. That is all wrapped up in his name and he lives out every letter. Charles k(no)ws exactly who he *is*. The benefit to this is being ever clear on who he *is not*. His free spirit allows him to say yes to many things, but at the flip of a switch his intuitive nature allows him to give a clear, firm or resistant "no" anytime he senses that he or our family is being pulled in a direction that is not best for us. You may be now asking, "what's the point of all of this?" The name is the point.

Your name—it is a guide to push the limits. Think of any brand name—a random one. As quickly as you identify what it is known for you can just as easily identify the list of things that name will never be known for or associated with. A brand name clearly, cleverly and competitively eliminates any alternatives to what the brand intentionally and strategically wishes to be known for. By defining who they are they have made clear for themselves who they are not. The power of their name is in being able to say no to anything that is contrary to their goal and it gives them the gift of direction. The name gives them a sense of direction. The name gives them the rights to create the personal-reality, the image that they want to see of themselves in the world and the image that the world will have to see.

Use these statements to declare your worth and to combat any phrase or action that seeks to limit your value or steal your power. You have the power to say no to anything that threatens or challenges your new positioning statement. If it does not meet you at your worth then it is not worth saying yes to. That will give you integrity and will keep you from selling yourself below your value. This integrity will become your brand and your reputation.

Any time you say no to what does not align with your positioning statement you are saying yes to the potential for anything that does. Imagine the profound impact this will have on your life and your relationships. You may attract new faces that will be genuinely intrigued by your new vision. You will command a new respect for yourself, for others and from others. You will no longer settle for the limits that others put upon you. It will cause a separation between what others may have grown comfortable with in their knowledge of you but that is no matter. *The goal* is not comfort. *The goal* is to leave this life, having given all that you had to give, to transfer the gift of direction into everything that you encountered pushing them to *the ultimate goal*.

LIVE THE PRE-SENT

Albert Einstein has been credited with stating, "the true sign of intelligence is not knowledge but *imagination*." This word contains within it the infinity of possibility. Nothing is impossible to the imagination. Your imagination can give you a look into your future and insight into how to make that imaginative future your present. It is said that the present is a gift. If that is true then it must have been a gift that was given prior to your receiving it. That suggests that your present is *pre-sent*. Think about the implications for a second. The reality that you are encountering today the limitations that you are experiencing, the joy, frustration, peace, failure or even successes are all pre-sent constructs of your own imagination.

We are intelligent enough to comprehend that things do come up but they are still in many cases, influenced by our imagination. We imagine that we are safe or vice versa. We imagine that we will win or vice versa. Let us not get into semantics here. We are not explaining away terrible things or undermining or devaluing experiences fully outside of our control. However as we are discussing the present, whether we are present or not is within our control. Determining the outcome is not always in our control. When we trust someone or something it is our imagination that creates the perception that gives us the necessary security to trust them. Our imagination is what we use to fill in the gaps that uphold the belief we have in it him, her or them. The power of imagination is often overlooked as a limiting factor of where you can and cannot go, of what you can or cannot do, of what you will or will not become. *Imagination*.

If you are convinced that your situation will never change then you cannot expect it to. If you are only imagining all of the things that can go wrong then you may never experience all of the things that could go right or you reduce the joy that you would experience along the way to finding either. If you do not believe that your life will ever amount to anything then most likely it will not amount to all that it could. If you truly believe that you are not worthy to live out the fullness of your potential to embrace your passion and project that power through propulsion, you will wake up receiving the present of submaximal living. If someone or something is dominating your life and you feel inferior to it or them, then they will remain as such. If you are always afraid to take the flight of your life then you will continue to live below your potential to propel yourself or others.

Your current circumstances are the presents that you pre-sent being re-presented to you in the present. Read that last line again very slowly. We hope you like your gift. Eventually there comes a point where you grow tired of opening the same present each day pretending to act surprised that it is exactly like the last day. That is foolishness. Change the pre-sent. You have been given authority as CEO of *you*. You have the ability to say no in accordance with who you want to become so that you may say yes to who that person may be. You have the propulsive power to change today what you ordinarily would have pre-sent to tomorrow.

If you have watched the film *Back to the Future*, you may recall how it dealt with the notion of subtle change having the power to impact the future drastically. Imagination is the same. It is not the same as a daydream. It is a power that comes with knowing *the goal* and embracing the gift of direction in you. With these two things comes an authority to move forward and to move things forward. Imagine what might happen if you were to renew your mind through actively engaging your imagination and then working toward that vision. It is the same process that gives us our fashion, our vehicles, inventions. They all started in the imagination. Then came the prototype, the trials, the revisions, the funding, the release, the adoption, the acceptance, the employees, the company, the profit. Literally all started in the imagination. Some people have literally drawn their imagination on a piece of napkin at a bar and it has grown into a multimillion operation that propels culture, communities and countries. There is no limit to the imagination but if you are not imagining *what if* now you will look back and ask *what if* then.

Afraid? So what. Do it afraid. If the possibility of your imagination does not scare you then it is not large enough. As we have been sure to make very clear we are advocating a purpose that is bigger than you are or may be, but that should not stop you from pushing forward. The quote we often hear told to children is, "aim for the moon. Even if you miss, you will land amongst the stars." Pushing your limits requires this imaginative thinking. *Set your mind on things above not earthly things.* See beyond the impact you can have in one lifetime. *Whatever is true, whatever wins respect, whatever is just, whatever is pure, whatever is lovable, whatever is of good repute...if there is any virtue or anything regarded worthy of praise, cherish the thought of these things.* That is how you push your limits and embrace the power of propulsion. Imagination will inspire you to *throw off any weight or self-inflicted nonsense* that would hinder the power of propulsion in your life.

As children we are always following our creative impulses, our potential. We are young and oblivious to *how life works*. Those who are currently doing the unthinkable and the impossible have never given up their ability to live beyond *how life works*. In the movie *Coming to America* one of the most famous lines by King Jaffe Joffer was "who told you that?" Trust us, it is much funnier in the film and raises the question and tone that you should ask yourself when what you imagine is threatened with thoughts that say it will never work. Who told you that? Who cares if it is improbable? *I am* probable. Who cares if it seems impossible? *I am* possible. *Anything is possible to someone who believes*. This is living on the edge pushing the limits, pushing the boundaries. This is seeing life like a child. This is seeing the world as your playground. This is the secret passage way back into the kingdom.

Maybe when you were younger you thought everything was possible. Then you began to grow and became conditioned to begin accepting limits above living. When we were kids we possessed the skill of activating our imagination. You drew out sometimes literally, the power to change the course of your life at any given second. Everything you created was a masterpiece. Every game was a championship game. Every meal was the best you had ever made. Everything was an adventure. Even if you did not grow up in a safe environment or loving home, you still had something. We lived in suspended disbelief. Life was limitless. If no one ever said to you that you could become anything that you wanted to be or achieve anything that you wanted to achieve you would still believe it were possible. If nothing around us changed, at any moment we would change ourselves on the inside. Are you understanding? There is a difference between childish and childlike. Childlike is the secret to pushing your limits.

THE FLIGHT OF YOUR LIFE

As actors Yvana and I have trained with a few great names in the industry. One of the greatest things we have embraced is the ability to *play*. Playfulness can accelerate you in every area of your life. Even the most mundane tasks can become a little less drum if it were to become a game. Life is in fact, a game. Some people are playing it better than others but there is no doubt that those who see it as a game have an advantage over those who cannot see it. Those who still live by the concept of coloring outside of the lines find it much easier to think outside of the box. These terms are not business terms, they are playground terms.

Before you understood that crayons were made to color within lines you could not help but to stay true to yourself. Sometimes, you would intentionally scribble colors that did not make sense even if you knew better. Sometimes you would intentionally color outside of the lines and scribble all over the paper because you were inspired to follow the joy of the journey to creation, which is the originally designed function of the challenge. The lines were and will always be guidelines, not rules that govern creativity. Even now as an adult there are artists whose paintings and drawings literally look like a two-year-old created them and they are worth thousands. The greatest athletes, greatest performers, greatest influencers, greatest at anything never lost this ability to live their imagination. What is different is that they *choose* every day to live in what is possible instead of what is presented.

If you happen to be five feet tall it may not be for you to expect to be drafted into the NBA, but that should never stop you from working as if it could happen at any moment. As you may recall the determined destination is not *the goal*. Your determination, discipline and drive may propel you to a platform that you were not expecting along the way. However if you do not take your shot, you will have missed the probable and the improbable. Yvana dreamed of making the Brazil Olympics in particular and worked hard for her athleticism and disciplined herself to get a shot. Yvana took the shot and though the federation did not back her after winning a championship, she would have never seen the opportunity to be flown to Brazil, staying in Brazil for a week and filming a short film in Brazil; it later became an international commercial for a large premium brand. Yvana would have never known that being associated with a premium brand would later line her up to travel internationally as a brand ambassador and presenter for one of the world's premium luxury brands.

I had no clue that after suffering a career-ending injury I would marry the girl that I had met a year prior, move to be with her and become her coach. I did not know that my desire to make her the best hurdler she could be would lead me to earn multiple certifications, train other professional athletes, have a thriving business and help me to earn multiple master's degrees. Keep going after your dreams because like all dreams they are communicating something to you. Whether the dream is literal or figurative you have to pursue it and propel yourself in the direction of that dream. You will never know what is meant for you along the way.

Play more to propel further. If your job is to process payments, start making it a game to see how many you can complete in an hour. Set a certain number of transactions as your inspiration by the end of day and find a friend who may be willing to play along with you. Each week whoever wins has to buy the other one of their favorite treats. If you are an athlete imagine yourself standing on the podium with your hands raised high. Imagine that every run, every rep is for the championship. If you get this lift, you are the champion. If you hit this turn, you are the champion. It is very simple yet if you are honest, you will admit just how difficult it may have been since laying your imagination to rest. You will soon notice that the things that seemed to cause you the most resistance are actually accelerating your progress. You will begin to see that your work—but ultimately your worth—has significance and meaning. You will look back and realize that each day you have pre-sent a new outlook and new possibilities and are presenting the image that you want others to see.

MAKE YOUR MOVE

Good things may come to those who wait but are experienced by those who make their move to own them. An opportunity may be right in front of you but it is not truly yours unless you *pursue* it. Period. No matter how long you wait opportunities will come and they will go. If you have the faith to see things *come to pass* that is exactly what they will do if you do not make your move. They will have come—to pass. That is the tragic reality of refusing to make your move. Active passivity is still inactivity.

You may have heard a version of the story of *The Man Who Drowned,* which has been paraphrased into many versions and jokes but the messages remain:

> A man was stuck on a rooftop in a flood. He was praying to God for help. Soon a rowboat came by and someone shouted, "jump in! I can save you." The man shouted back, "no, it's okay! I'm praying to God. He is going to save me." So the rowboat went on. Then a motorboat came by. The driver shouted, "jump in! I can save you." To this the man said, "no, thanks. I'll be okay. I'm praying for God to save me." So the motorboat went on. Then

a helicopter came by, and the pilot shouted down, "grab this rope, and I will lift you to safety." To this the stranded person again replied, "no, I have enough faith to believe that God is going to save me." So the helicopter reluctantly flew away leaving him on the roof. The water continued to rise until it reached above the rooftop and the man drowned. Having died he now stood before God and took the chance to try this case with God. "I had faith in you but you did not save me. *You* let me drown. I cannot understand why!" To this, God replied, "I sent *you* a rowboat, a motorboat and a helicopter."

Faith can move mountains but you have to walk the distance to get to the other side. If the mountain moves and you do not, the only thing that will change is the view. Faith is powerful enough to bring opportunities to you but powerless if you are not ready to make your move. *Faith without work(s) is dead.* Do not get this twisted though, this goes two ways. Works without faith are dead also. God did not let the man in the story drown and neither did the people who were propelled to save him. His faith was alive but he was as good as dead because he did not make *his* move. You cannot blame anyone else for the actions you did not take or the moves that you did not make. Ownership.

On the other side of this story is how his inactivity affected the people who had been *sent* to save him. This is what many will miss in reading this story. What is best for you is best for others. Had the man made his move and been rescued the person in the rowboat, the motorboat

> Faith can move mountains but you have to walk the distance to get to the other side.

THE FLIGHT OF YOUR LIFE

or the helicopter would have been a hero and likely become a friend. Unfortunately when we do not make a move, we impede upon the propulsion of those whose purpose had propelled them our direction. His inactivity would also impact the way those would-be rescuers would see themselves and likely the way they would perceive faith. Remember how we began this book? Energy released never ends. It will continue to make waves long beyond the moment. This is why we encourage you today—make *your* move, the one that is actually best for you.

We understand. You may be reading this book and have just gone through or are enduring something that is truly devastating but you have to make your move. You may feel as though you are in way over your head but you cannot sit there and drown in your feelings or vices until you drown. Make your move. You may be in so much debt that you literally can feel the weight and pressure but doing nothing will not make the problem go away. You are going to have to face it one penny at a time so make your move.

You may even know what move needs to be made but you will not commit to it. You build yourself up, muster the courage, stand at the edge and...nothing. You procrastinate and further delay your moment to move until the moment passes you by. When I was a child my dad would take me to the local natatorium. I remember eyeing the high dive and thinking that was not so high. It did not appear all that intimidating from afar and I was a bit of a daredevil, this would be nothing. I remember walking myself all of the way to the deep end nodding to the lifeguard like, "you know what I am about to do," and I would begin to climb the ladder. I never understood how the ladder seemed to extend the higher I climbed up. It literally felt like I was in the sky about to fall to my death. The high dive is not intimidating until you complete the climb and step out past the handrails on the board.

I can remember looking up and watching birds fly by my head and then looking down and seeing a bottomless pit beneath me at least a few thousand feet down. The fact that this indoor pool was extremely well cared for and the water was extremely clear did not help at all. If the water was brown, it would not have looked that far down. I know some of you are concerned but I grew up in Mississippi, brown water can be clean. I clearly remember attempting to turn around and walking back toward the ladder to climb down. I remember turning around and seeing the other kids standing behind me waiting for me to jump. First off, no one was even interested in the high dive until I dared myself to do it and second, there is no second.

Before I could walk back to reach the handrails I remember hearing the annoying whistle of the very same lifeguard. There was no turning back. My terror pertains to you in this way. You are already where you are so just make your move. There are people waiting on you. If you do not make your move they cannot make theirs. There are others who are counting on you to finish and will draw their inspiration from seeing you do it. There are people who need to see you commit and propel off into the deep end. The feelings and emotions are all real but you have to commit and make your move. You need to get out of your feelings and focus on flying. You know exactly what we are saying to you.

Make the move that you should make or do not make it at all. Leave no room for hesitation. My mother Annie, is an excellent driver. Although I was naturally good at keeping myself safe she taught me so many little things that have helped keep me from hurt, harm or danger. One rule in particular that I remember is with regard to entering the freeway. My mother would always remind me to signal, check my mirrors, turn my head and see. Then she would be absolutely clear to remind me to *make my move and to not hesitate* so

THE FLIGHT OF YOUR LIFE

I would not cause an accident. The risk of failure is greatest when you hesitate. If you do not make *your* move you may interfere with the forward progress of those around you or cause them to run into you.

Whenever I fly I try to take note of all of the flights coming in as well as those flights that are going out even after I board the airplane. I listen for the pilot to address the crew to notify them of what number our departure falls. I am always fascinated by the volume of how many planes are synchronized to the minute in ascent and descent. I am especially amazed when I fly in and out of international airports like JFK, DFW, ATL or LAX. It boggles my mind to think of the impact of one delay and how it can set the remainder of the day off course for thousands of travelers.

Upon announcing clearance for takeoff I am often exhilarated as the plane suddenly begins to accelerate. There is no slow roll buildup it feels like maximum propulsion, full throttle. At that moment you know that there is no backing out of this one. You are along for this ride no matter what and your pilot is locked in and committed whether you are or not. It is much like the feeling you might get on a roller coaster with a reputation for speed. I am both proud and amazed at the nerve that pilots have to commit, make a move and take to the skies without hesitation. Once their opportunity comes, they make a move, push the limit and fly. That is the lesson.

Boss up. You will no longer accept anything that does not meet you at your worth. You will pre-sent yourself a present worth living. Put yourself in propulsive position and make your move. Whatever the move is make it. Commit to it and trust the process. If it means sacrificing some wants, sacrifice them. If it means purchasing an expensive training course, getting a coach or attending a seminar, then do it. Whatever your move is it should scare you a little; it should cost something. Change does not come cheaply. It also does not always mean quitting a relationship, team or company. Whatever your move it is time to push the limit and make one.

Believe in yourself, bet on you and double down. *The goal* is not the path but it is the door. You must make a move and walk through it. Register for that online course this week. Sign up for the six-month package with a professional coach or personal trainer. Put your name in the hat for that promotion opportunity. Connect with that business coach you have been following online for months. Make your move and remind yourself that you can never lose by investing in yourself. You are putting yourself in propulsive position to push the limit. That is not the same as maxing out your limits. As CEO of *you*, having a business mentality and mindset means knowing when to make sacrifices or budget cuts if necessary to ensure that your company does not go under like the man who drowned. Look for ways to leverage or reallocate resources that will allow you the opportunity to make your move. Your company may have a tuition reimbursement program. You may be eligible for a small business loan. If these are not relative to your circumstance make use of the principle by making the move that will help you go fast and eventually go as far as you would dream.

GO THE FASTEST

You may have heard a version of this African proverb: "if you want to go fast, go alone. If you want to go far, go together." This quote is often misinterpreted and misused to devalue those who would go alone. The statement offers multiple levels of wisdom and limiting it to any one interpretation would be shortsighted. *For everything there is an appointed time and an appropriate time for every activity on earth.* That means there is a time for going alone and a time for going

THE FLIGHT OF YOUR LIFE

together. There is a time for going fast and a time for going more slowly. The point is propulsion is still occurring. This relates to everything and points back to specificity. There is a specific reason for being able to access the liberty and power to do either. Limiting yourself to either way of thinking is a disservice and can cause more damage than good. The ability to change the pace or to do some things alone and other things together is the glory of being able to push limits. They are all interchangeable and interwoven.

It has always amazed me how quickly this quote would be whipped out and thrown on the table like a trump card as though going fast or going far are mutually and morally exclusive. As former track athletes Yvana and I still keep our eyes on the sport and even catch the occasional endurance event. I can remember the hype around the 2019 Vienna City Marathon as runner Eliud Kipchoge was to attempt completing the marathon in under two hours. This feat was coined as the "last barrier of modern athletics" by some. It was reminiscent of the impact of the first sub-ten-second one-hundred-meter sprint or the first four-minute mile. At the time the world actually believed to run that far and to run that fast would make a human heart explode. As with all running events, the speeds at which competitors are able to push the limits and run distances once seen as distance races is changing the context of what speed, sprinting and endurance looks like. To run 26.2 miles in under two hours requires running fast and far simultaneously and challenges the idea of speed. In order to push the limit, lose this quote. The quote is not discussing limits but the limitlessness of possibility and the accessibility to do anything.

As we look at modern technology there are thousands of individuals and thousands of things that can do all three—*go fast*, go far and go together. There are also things that do one thing better than another by design. There are very fast things that are made specifically to transport slower ones and there are slow things made to transport faster things. Propulsion is a balanced art of making the necessary adjustments, accommodating to the needs of a purpose and using the best means of meeting *the goal*. It is irresponsible to assume or presume that one is greater than the other or in some way does not benefit the other.

A further look into this statement also reveals a gem of wisdom. It is saying that no one gets anywhere without the help of others. Even if you are the greatest athlete without a coach or a team, you would not have a platform to be seen. This is absolutely true. We are all standing on the shoulders of those who came before us. We are standing on the soil of souls who made sacrifices in order to propel us one step further toward a determined destination they would never see. There are lives that came before us who would not see any of the freedoms that some of us live openly today but they were committed to pushing us forward even if they themselves could go no further—even if it meant going alone. Their faith and action worked to see us alive today. This is especially true for African Americans, minorities in the United States and other countries that have suffered under the many tragedies of colonialism.

When we consider going fast and going far we must also consider that the work of those who worked together to make fast happen do not always get the chance to go far. A team of engineers and scientists may design the fastest vehicle in history but the fame goes to the individual who goes fast. A team may create but it is often the individual that achieves it. NASA has been credited with putting a man on the moon but the glory belongs to the first man who made it there. The proverb is about the needed result and the result determines the method.

THE FLIGHT OF YOUR LIFE

As an encouragement to you if you are in a season where you need absolute speed, go fast. Not recklessly or aimlessly but honorably as a tribute to those who have contributed to your ability to do so. Go fast because of what it means to those whose sacrifices of time, energy and resources ensured that you were equipped to handle those speeds. As an encouragement to you if you are in a season that requires patience and endurance, stay the course and go as far as you can because your work is moving a mass much bigger than yourself. You are moving ever so slightly toward *the goal*. If you are in a season where you are constantly managing speed and endurance go fast and as far as you can because you are the embodiment of all the hopes and dreams of those who you came from and those who may come from you.

Anything that goes fast can still go far. Do not ascribe to the limit of thinking that going alone is always rooted in selfish ambition or that if it goes fast it does not impact or increase togetherness. A great father will go to great lengths and at even greater speeds to ensure that his family is safe and is provided for. A great mother will go to great lengths and at even greater speeds to ensure that her family is safe and is provided for. A great spouse will go to great lengths and at even greater speeds to ensure that their family is safe and provided for. Going together may actually mean going alone in order for *together* to remain a possibility.

The proverb is also a wise expression of sequencing. These are steps to success. Going alone or going fast will inspire others to run alongside you. When you have a clear understanding of your divine authority know your worth and accept nothing less, leave and live a better pre-sent each day and make your moves with confidence and courage; others will want to partner with that. Seeing others come alongside you will energize your steps and will help you to keep moving forward. Eventually you will have forgotten all about the pain of running by yourself and will begin running for everyone else running with you. It will encourage you to know that there are people running with you as long as they are behind you, they will keep pushing you forward in such a way that the momentum generated from the back will transfer to the front and push you forward.

No one is being pulled. Everyone is pushing forward, covering ground, taking new territory, reaching new heights and creating new landmarks. For those of you in leadership positions remember this proverb. It contains great perspectives and can serve as a reminder that you too, once went alone and now that there are people behind you. Do not forget who is propelling your career. You are not pulling your team, they are pushing you. If you are pulling them then you are not propelling them, you are compelling them. If you are a coach remember this proverb. It contains great perspectives and can serve as a reminder that you too, once went alone and now that there is a team behind you do not forget who is propelling your career. If you are a company remember this proverb. It contains great perspectives and can serve as a reminder that you too once went alone and now that there is a customer base behind you, do not forget who is propelling your corporation. The wind at your back cannot be generated by you so be sure to always respect and honor those who are keeping you in the front.

Proverbs give insight into the magnitude and impact that your determination to push the limit may have on objects much larger than you. Eventually there will come a point, if you focus on what and who propels you forward, that the movement that you and those with you will create will push culture forward. It will literally possess the power to change the landscape of an entire landmass. It will positively propel the whole of whatever it comes in contact with. It will become

THE FLIGHT OF YOUR LIFE

so large that smaller objects can no longer resist the positive and inspired direction that you and all of the people are headed. The momentum will be so powerful that only the movement will remain. You will have given the gift of direction to more people than you would have imagined.

Going together may actually mean going alone

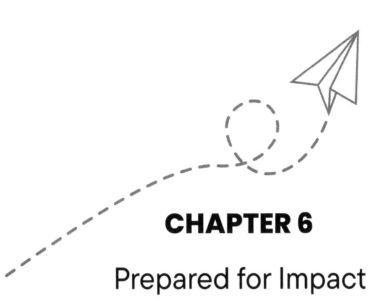

CHAPTER 6

Prepared for Impact

Someone once said that landing a plane is a controlled crash without the big explosion at the end. This is a bit dramatic but there is a solid point to be made. What goes up must come down and whatever comes down will make an *impact*. We typically think of the act of landing as a smooth transition from air to ground but what we may not comprehend or appreciate is how our entire flight began with the end in mind. The only objective is to touch down and safely get you to where you need to *be*. The flight of your life will be no different. Before making impact there will have been multiple communications, hundreds of considerations and thousands of calculations made before impact. All of these things work together to ensure that you reach your determined destination in sight and that when impact is made it would be seamless and routine. You may have even had the pleasure of a perfect landing where the pilot lands a plane so smoothly that the impact is made before you even notice.

You too, should be preparing for impact or more conscious of the impact that you are already having. You cannot

THE FLIGHT OF YOUR LIFE

deny impact and inactivity will only delay it. Whether you like it or not the dreams, goals and aspirations that you are propelling toward and the ones that you feel compelled to abandon have a lasting impact on yourself and others. Yvana and I definitely want you to achieve all of your personal goals and we hope that we are inspiring you to take the necessary action into establishing and reaching them. However if you do not understand your *why* behind your *what*, you may lose *the way*.

We hope that we have helped you to this point in our offering of practical insights in a nontraditional way. You can immediately apply many of the things we have presented to you and make some serious gains in whatever area you desire. We want nothing more than to help you to see beyond those goals as they are not *the goal*. We want you to live with the knowledge and respect of how valuable your life is and the fullness of the impact you could have. We also want to make you fully aware of the power that you possess to make an impact and we hope to do so by further impacting yours. When we talk about preparing for impact we are referencing the culmination of all that you are, all that you are becoming and all that you will be. Being prepared for this will give meaning to the flight of your life and will give power to whatever it was that led you to read this book.

There is so much in store for you that we can hardly wait to share these final thoughts with you. We know that as we receive the privilege and honor of making an impact upon you, you will have an even greater impact on every person that encounters you. You may have picked up our book with expectations of reading pages full of random clichés and anecdotes that would stroke your ego. You may have opened these pages having expected us to give you step-by-step instructions on

> You cannot deny impact and inactivity will only delay it.

how to increase your happiness, earnings or athletic performance. We hope that throughout this entire experience you are seeing that none of those things are independent in nature. By that we mean we hope that having made it this far, you are seeing with greater clarity the power that you already have to use your resources to put yourself in a propulsive position for the purpose of putting others in theirs.

    This is what you are made for; this is what all of this living is about. Every point and every person in your life has been preparing you for impact—even the ones who were hoping to hinder your ability to make one. All of your past experiences are tools to propel you to progress, even the painful moments that you pushed through and are still pushing through. Those moments that felt as though you were enduring something purposeless you will come to better understand, all has purpose. Your purpose is propelling you whether you know it, recognize it, care to see it or not. Purpose will always propel because your purpose is propulsion. We will discuss this more in depth as we make our final descent, but for now we will get back to the topic at hand.

    Each phase that you have read through has been our attempt to propel you into taking ownership of your purpose and to prepare you for impact. These six chapters are written in direct respect to the six phases of flight. We have focused our efforts on activating your purpose by introducing it to you in pieces that you can easily put together for maximum impact. The biblical wisdom, insights from applied sciences and business strategies could give you the tools to assess where you are in comparison to where you want to be. At each stage we purposefully introduced you to one phase of flight. We have discussed topics that cover *planning*, *confirmation*, *taxiing or transition*, *takeoff* and *cruising*. And now we will spend the remainder of our time on revealing to you how you have been prepared to make an impact.

THE FLIGHT OF YOUR LIFE

Our entire focus from the beginning was to help you connect to the impetus of taking flight and to do so with a particular intent. As you may now recognize intent *is* the power within purpose. Your intent should always be not only taking flight but inspiring as many people as possible to take flight. The purpose of your existence impacts everything connected to it. You may never know how the flight of your life will propel future generations, families and children of children. The path that your persistence will pave may not bring you present praise but you *progress* people, and that is the greatest impact you can have.

A journey that would have taken weeks can be completed in days. Letters sent in love or great urgency could arrive on time, not a moment too late or too soon. The flight of your life will create progress in systems, how people see themselves and others. It will impact cultures and environments. You can have this type of impact. You were made for this type of influence. You are prepared to live a life and leave a legacy of propulsion. You have been pre- *paired* for this.

Our encouragement to you is to start now. It does not matter where you start if the start is rough or ugly. It does not matter if you think the task is too small or the impact is too great. Just start. It does not matter if you are sure or confident. Start. Start small, start somewhere but at all costs, start. *Do not despise small beginnings for the Lord rejoices to see the work beginning.* You are not doing it for the praise of people, you are doing it for the propulsion of people. You are becoming an influencer of cultures. Begin propelling someone or something with who you are *becoming*. Whatever you are hoping to become you must first *be*. Start with the people who are nearest, the circles and environments that you are in now.

Look for ways that you can create momentum in the life of someone else. Make every effort to avoid allowing limited biases to get in the way of your impact. You will never know which impact will be greatest or which will yield the greatest dividends or return. A few life verses that come to mind informs:

> *Those who water, will be watered...Give and it will come back to you...What a man sows, he reaps...Do to others what you would have them do to you...Your abundance being a supply for their need, so that their abundance also may become a supply for your need, that there may be equality.*

As you become more intentional seeing and sowing purpose, you will become more proficient at making impacts that will grow exponentially over time. Every impact creates opportunity to make even bigger ones. Consider where you could begin making a propulsive impact where you are currently. Ask yourself if you have actually made any sincere effort to make an impact in what or who seems to be insignificant. *Whoever can be trusted with a little can be trusted with a lot.* If you are truly ready to take the flight of your life you will realize the critical importance of preparing for impact and being prepared for impact. Keep your eyes open for places and people where you can make an impact even if it goes unnoticed.

GENERATE IT

You have been given an irrevocable gift. None of us opted to be here but nonetheless, it was determined that we should *be*. You were made to *be*. That is what makes you a living *be-ing*. This will make more sense as we work through what this means. You now know that propulsion is the purpose of

THE FLIGHT OF YOUR LIFE

all living things. You were made to be a propulsive force in every area—in all that you do and wherever you *are*. For the next few moments we will drill down on this principle until the implications impact you at your core. We will look deeper into the face value of words that will make this pivotal and particularly significant point clear.

You may have even picked up on some of the wordplay and italicized and emphasized letters already. Particularly you may have noticed that we have added emphasis to forms of the word *be*. The word *be* is particularly powerful as it corrects the frame and cleans the mirror that allows you to see the image that you bear. *Be* speaks to all that you were made to accomplish and places an eternal weight and gravitas to any and every goal, endeavor, desire, place, position or status that you possess. Take a look at these definitions found in the *Merriam-Webster* dictionary of the word *be*:

> *to equal in meaning : have the same connotation as : to symbolize*
>
> *to have identity with : to constitute the same idea or object as*
>
> *to constitute the same class as*
>
> *to have a specified qualification or characterization*
>
> *to belong to the class of*
>
> *to have an objective existence : have reality or actuality : to live*
>
> *to have, maintain, or occupy a place, situation, or position*
>
> *to remain undisturbed or uninterrupted*
>
> *to take place : occur*

to come or go

Be empowers all that you are by giving whatever it is that you hope to accomplish—its meaning. *Be* empowers the identity of who you would hope to be and what you would like to see in this world. *Be* empowers all that you were prepared to accomplish by giving it class, character and a focused objective. In whatever space or position you choose to occupy you have a right to remain undisturbed and uninterrupted while disrupting the status quo. *Be* empowers you to make things happen that need to or when things do occur. *Be* is the freedom to be-coming or going.

Maybe you have put so much emphasis on accomplishing your goals that you fail to realize that goals accomplished are the *output* of your *being*. When you are dedicated to investing your entire *being* toward *be*-coming you will *be* what is *coming*. Remember this from previous topics: *As a person thinks, so is he.* We hope that you do not miss the power in what we just said. Your *being* literally propels what you are *believing* toward you. This implies that it is in the process of coming to *be, hence be-come*. Your entire existence is based upon propulsion. That is all that life is meant to teach you. You truly become what you believe yourself to be. This is why everything that compels you wants to pull you far from who you are meant to be in order that you would *be*-come or manifest something different.

Your *being constitutes* meaning. You have the propulsive power to make things matter. You have identity and class. You have the propulsive power to raise the bar to higher standards. Your *being constitutes* qualification. You have the propulsive power to walk in divine authority and, if necessary, declare your ability to earn any certification necessary to validate what you are. Your *being constitutes* characterization. You

> Your being literally propels what you are believing toward you.

have the propulsive power to bring life, energy and artistic creativity and representation of humanity into every environment. Your *being constitutes* belonging. You have the propulsive power to change hearts through fostering close and intimate relationships. Your *being constitutes* an objective existence. You have the propulsive power to declare, define and deliver any goal with purpose and intent. Your *being constitutes* position and a right to occupancy. You have the propulsive power to take up space unapologetically and to create room for others. Your *being constitutes* continuity. You have the propulsive power to access a consistent flow of resource and provision and to be one. Your *being constitutes* occurrence. You have the propulsive power to innovate, to make things happen or to create the right moment if necessary. Your *being constitutes* the freedom to come and to go. You have the propulsive power to create movement and momentum as you wish with or without permission.

    Since you were prepared for impact made in the image and likeness of The Supreme *Being*, that makes you not only a replica but a replicator of what must be. You are a *generator*. Your being possesses the ability to create, to duplicate and to convert dynamic power into propulsion. This is what we have meant by having the gift of direction. It is a signature of the designer that has been given to you that you would *be* in this world. This is why we were intentional in our effort to keep you from limiting your thinking to see any particular job, function, title, personal or performance goal as *the goal*. The endeavors you entertain, the functions or roles that you hold or the desires you were after are vehicles of purpose for your choosing. More profoundly the vehicle of purpose that eternity chose to make an impact on earth, in your country, state, city, community, company or team is you.

You are a generator of power also known as a *propulsor*. You are a living, moving, breathing *be*ing prepared for impact. Generate one. You were created for a purpose, with a purpose and by purpose. Your being presents the image of the Supreme Being. You were pre-sent to propel, to be fruitful and to multiply everything and in everything. A generator can produce a particular outcome on demand. Like the goose that lays golden eggs you are invaluable and have the power to use your propulsive power to create impact in any lane that you wish to—just pick one and push for it. This is why we encourage you to remove the limits to what you can be; you can generate almost anything. Take a look at this short list of synonyms and words that are related to the word *generator*:

Author	Founding-	Builder	Developer	Maker	Promoter
Begetter	father	Co-Creator	Deviser	Pioneer	Encourager
Creator	Inaugurator	Co-Founder	Formulator	Producer	Galvanizer
Establisher	Initiator	Conceiver	Innovator	Researcher	Inspiration
Father	Instituter	Contriver	Introducer	Researchist	Inspirer
Founder	Originator	Designer	Inventor	Organizer	Sire

If you skimmed through this list please take a moment to read through it again. Only this time read it knowing that at any point in time any of these things are in you. These are not professions, roles or job titles. These are in you— your *be*ing. You are valuable. You are powerful enough to propel entire industries and people. You can generate the impact that you desire to have because you are made in the image of the Creator. Grasp the impact that you can have. If somehow you have been compelled to believe that you are not capable, are unworthy or have no connection to these things, make the choice to see what could be and generate it. You can reclaim your power any time by simply choosing to *be*. If you have been going the wrong way, remember all it takes is you to regrasp the truth of what you were made to be. At any point you can generate a fundamental change in form, character and function. You can generate a change in how you think, see yourself, your purpose and *the goal*. That has always been power available to you. That power is *conversion*.

The power to generate is the power to convert. You are a convertible. Your power may have been taken from you, given away or lost. But at the moment that you accept conversion, the Source of power will enter into everything that you do and will help you to convert others along the way who have misplaced their potential, power and purpose. When people who do not believe in what is possible see you, they will believe that all things are possible. When people do not have the faith, they will see you and you will increase their faith. When people need hope they will see you and receive hope. When someone has a heavy heart, they will see you and their heart will be lifted. You will convert hearts and minds. You generating all that you could ever become for others to see makes it become real. You are prepared for impact.

BECOME IT

My wife is an extraordinary woman. She has a unique gift of prophecy and a connection with God that I am often inspired by. She teaches me things every day about myself and about her, but most importantly about the principles that you are reading in this book. When I met Yvana I was a young marketing specialist who would wear a suit and tie to a baby shower. She came into my life and everything changed. I was always in corporate mode. It was the vision that I had for my life because I assumed life could be found in a cubicle or corner office. I was not afraid to settle in a career for the long run. I had no aspirations to travel or to try new things. I was bland in appearance despite my personality being so big.

Earlier we shared a story of Yvana's dream of competing at the Rio Olympics. We also shared the story of how broken she was to learn despite having qualified and winning a federation title that politics would prevent her from making a trip to the Olympic Games. You may recall pieces of this story but what we want to highlight is just how strongly she envisioned herself to be a world-class athlete competing in Brazil. She would regularly envision herself standing in Brazil with fans all around, lights centered on her and becoming the focus of international recognition. Every day Yvana would believe, *be* and *live* her conviction that the moment was going to be hers. When the Olympics had come and gone and the hurt and confusion remained all that was left was her belief. She could comprehend that something had changed but she did not give up on her belief. Nor did I.

She could have quit everything and thrown in the towel. She could have let doubt and fear steal her power to generate direction and shut everything down that even resembled the life that she hoped was ahead of her but she would not let it go. We continued to train and figured that we might continue the long road of pursuing the dream for a few more years. She competed for another year and was eventually invited to join the European circuit. Her agent had called telling her that she was invited to compete in a few meets around Europe but we would have to get her there initially. She would have to earn her purse each week to continue the circuit until the end. Although this was not the dream it was good news, but something was not right about the opportunity. We had no idea where she would stay with no family or friends in Europe. I could not take time away from work to see to it that she remained safe. We were not afraid but we did not have peace and could certainly feel that if we had agreed to proceed, we would have been doing so under compulsion.

There were a few more tune-up meets before this circuit would begin, so we set our focus on a couple of weeks out. Yvana accepted an invitation to compete at one of them so we prepared accordingly. She was looking really good throughout the preparation for the meet so we felt confident going in. I had a strange feeling that I could not shake about this meet but it was too late. It was the day of the race and she had traveled alone. All I could do was pray against what I was being compelled to believe. I knew the time approximately that she would be running and I remember praying harder than ever for her safety and claiming a time for her that I had hoped she would see because she was so close to it that I felt confident that she was ready to run. A few hours later I heard from her expecting good news and instantly, my heart sank as she began to cry. She was running against some of the fastest hurdlers in the world and she was running on the heels of the leader and clipped a hurdle so hard that she tripped and fell, except this time when she fell she knew something was hurt. She told me that her shoulder has been dislocated and that she heard something pop in the back of her arm. An MRI confirmed that she had torn one of the muscles in her rotator cuff but that it could heal without surgery.

You may be thinking all of that faith, prayer and belief meant nothing. Well this is where the story gets really interesting. Before that meet Yvana and I had prayed and really asked God if sending her to Europe alone was the way in which she should go and if this was the path of propulsion that we needed to be on. We asked him in prayer to make no way for us to be able to accept the invitation if it was not going to be in her best. I am shocked now that I was not perceptive enough to know that God loves us so much that he will use whatever necessary to make his path known because this was the same prayer I had lifted up when I was making my semiprofessional debut as a track competitor years prior. My answer came in a ruptured Achilles tendon.

As if matters could not get any worse, Yvana was still able to run but she could not do so without pain. We were thinking that we might be able to survive the end of the season and had thought of the exposure or the potential of her running on the circuit would mean in future years. We were pretty sure that it was not the direction that we should go but Yvana and I are two people who can make things happen. The week that we were supposed to give her agent a definitive answer Yvana was involved in a car accident. A driver swerved after attempting to cut off traffic, jumped into her lane of oncoming traffic and totaled her vehicle. Yvana was alone and in pain. The driver was uninsured. Their passenger had warrants for their arrest and were about to flee the scene but Yvana sprinted across the seven lane highway and blocked the entrance where they were trying to escape until a state trooper and I arrived.

That was the official end to her season and would prove to be the end of her pursuit of athletics as a competitor. Yvana would undergo therapy and treatment for nearly nine months, was summoned to court for the accident, continued to train clients, connected with a clinical therapist and counselor, committed herself to keeping her fitness and physique and healed. All she wanted was to travel to Brazil to get her shot to compete for an international title—at the very least, to experience the lights, sounds, foods and culture. She had

THE FLIGHT OF YOUR LIFE

done everything that she needed to do to *be* in that moment and it looked like that moment would never be-come.

It was shortly after this time when I remember Yvana becoming obsessed with luggage. She would shop for luggage, look for luggage and literally try to convince me that she needed to buy luggage. She had nowhere to go at the time and had not been anywhere for an entire year and furthermore, we already had luggage. I remember thinking and sometimes passionately telling her that she did not need any new luggage. She kept telling me that she feels like she was going to be traveling all over the world and to new countries. At this point Yvana was not even working full time as she healed through the mental, physical and emotional pains that the year prior had brought upon her and us all at once. I told her that I was not going to be buying her any luggage, so she made a way to purchase her own brand-new luggage. She literally bought three new suitcases.

One day while I was off to work, Yvana received a casting notice and description for a short film for an unnamed client. She hears the voice of the Lord tell her to get up and to audition for a role. It was to play Laila Ali in a short film that would likely become an international commercial. She heard but she has had a series of bad circumstances that led her to doubt her hearing.

She heard the voice again: "audition for that role."

She heard but she has had a series of bad circumstances that led her to doubt her hearing.

She heard the voice again a third time, but this time with more urgency: "Yvana, audition for the role. Yvana, audition for the role, go upstairs, get Charles's weightlifting belt and boxing gloves and shorts, download the picture I am going to show you and submit yourself, the role is yours." Did I mention that Yvana heard but she had a series of bad circumstances that led her to doubt her hearing? That is until she heard it for the third time.

The casting team had been searching for someone who was around the age of Laila Ali when she had won her international boxing championship title. They wanted a person who not only looked like Laila but who was as fit as Laila was during the prime of her career and they had sent out a worldwide casting. The commercial would be filmed in various places including Brazil not far from where the Olympics had been held only a year prior.

You may remember how that story ends. Yvana auditioned online, not in person. Yvana and I went to our local gym and used our own fitness equipment, boxing gloves and pads to put together a boxing reel. You may remember that Yvana was taught to box at an early age and we would often use boxing as cross-training to keep her sprinting from becoming stale. Yvana and I submitted the tape and a few days later, Yvana Hepburn-Bailey received an ecstatic phone call from one of her agents that she booked the role and that she was selected from thousands of submissions across the world, not just the United States. It was shortly after they were negotiating rates, travel to and from the US, hotels, travel arrangements, local guides and the works. She was so fit that the production team had asked that for the next few weeks she would become a little softer to more closely resemble the young legend in the making.

Since Yvana was injured in her accident our legal counsel pursued the case and won. The amount awarded to Yvana was greater than the amount she had received in her entire track career and far outweighed the potential returns that she might have earned even if she were to have won each race during the European circuit. She would eventually fully recover from her injury and started booking right away in other commercials and theater opportunities.

THE FLIGHT OF YOUR LIFE

The following year Yvana was invited to interview to become an international brand presenter for one of the largest luxury vehicle manufacturers in the world. They loved her so much that they would bring her on to the team and start scheduling travel for her immediately after training. Almost suddenly she went from zero to one hundred. She was now traveling to New York, LA, Canada, Brazil, and many other states in between, some which she had never been to. I think you get the message. Everything that happened was pre-paired for her. Yvana had be-lieved so hard that what would be-*come*, be-*came*.

Please do not miss this. Even when it seems that everything is working against what you are trying to be, continue to be. Never give up on God because God is *the goal*. He is the giver of all life. Never give up on your direction because you are a generator of direction. Never give up on your belief because believing is your *be* living. By being all that she was Yvana was living what she would be until one day what was to be-*come*, be-*came*.

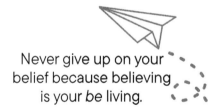

Never give up on your belief because believing is your *be* living.

REFLECT IT

You were made in the image of God. Eternity is in you and is meant to be reflected through you. If we were to ask you to tell us who you are, even if you were not yet sure of what you would say, the first two words would be, "I am." You would begin your thought with this because "I am" is the present participle of your existence, your *being-ness*. This is our point exactly. Everything that you would use to describe yourself would be a reflection of all that you are, who others see you to be, all that you have done and what you would like to do. The way you would give clarity of yourself to us would be to identify what you are at this current moment with respect given to all you are becoming. In other words you would try to communicate all that you are. If you said, "I am who I am," that would be enough. This encounter happens every day and mirrors the encounter given to us in the biblical conversation between Moses and God.

> You were made in the image of God. Eternity is in you and is meant to be reflected through you.

Israel as a nation, has a history of living under the compulsion of captivity. They needed a deliverer after having sojourned in Egypt for over four hundred years. When the time to be became, God introduced the purpose of propulsion to Moses. If you know anything about the life of Moses you will know that everything that led up to this point for him was part of a divine plan to prepare him for impact—his birth, how he would survive a death edict. He would be adopted by one of the daughters of the same ruler of Egypt who had ordered all children his age to be killed. How is that for a plot twist? He was educated and elevated as a prince of Egypt with great authority. There was no higher honor besides being the Pharaoh and if his story ended here, it would seem perfect, but there is more. Moses killed a man that was abusing a slave who was from the people that Moses had actually come from. Knowing that he could be put to death for murdering one of the servants to the Pharaoh, Moses escaped and lived in self-inflicted exile in the desert for forty years. He married and was content with

THE FLIGHT OF YOUR LIFE

living out the rest of his life in the desert with his family. What he did not know was that all of his life experiences were preparing him for impact even when it may have appeared to him that there was no impact to be made.

One day Moses encountered God in the desert. God revealed to him that he had a special purpose for him. He would be the one to propel his people out of compulsion of captivity. I love this moment of this story as God who could have simply made Moses do what he wanted, begins his statement with the word that means "to *come* and to *go*." He uses a form of the word *be* to give Moses freedom to choose although it would have ultimately resulted in the way that Moses had been pre-paired and prepared for.

Moses immediately responds to God by asking, "*who am I that I should...*" to which God responds, "*I will be* with you." Then Moses asks God what name he should give to the people whom he was to deliver as a sign that he had indeed been sent to rescue them. What happens here is the most interesting point of the entire conversation. Moses was concerned that the people would not only ask, "who are you?" but more importantly, "who is this God?" He was afraid that trying to tell them "the God of your Fathers" would not be good enough despite it being accurate. So Moses asked God to give him something; he never actually asks specifically for his name but rather, "what should I say to them?" God being in all things and in all places at the same time, responds without actually giving Moses a name. What he does gives him is a phrase. Christine Hayes professor of religious studies in classical Judaica at Yale University, offers insight on this in her own words:

> Moses says: "may I say who sent me?" He asks for God's name. "The Israelites will want to know who has sent me," and God replies

with a sentence, "Ehyeh asher ehyeh." This is a first person sentence that can be translated, "I am who I am," or perhaps, "I will be who I will be," or perhaps, "I cause to be what I cause to be." We really don't know but it has something to do with "being." So he asks who God is and God says, "I am who I am" or "I will cause to be what I will cause to be." So Moses wisely enough, converts that into a third-person formula: okay, he will be who he will be, he is who he is, "Yahweh asher Yahweh." God's answer to the question of his name is this sentence and Moses converts it from a first-person to a third-person sentence: he will be who he will be; he is who he is; he will cause to be.

Here is how the account relates to you. Your life is a likeness. It is a reflection of the fullness of what it means to *be*. Your *being* is a reflection of the Divine Being, the Most High Being, the Absolute Being, the One who will be and causes to be. When you live out your God-given purpose you are propelling into existence everything that will be, everything that he is and everything that he will cause to be. You are who you are. Unless you personally choose to deny that which he has made you to be, you will become all that he has made you to be and will propel others to be all that he has made them to be. You were prepared for impact and the flight of your life will make one. You must choose today what that impact will reflect and whose image that you want to see reflected—yours or his.

As you choose to accept this propulsive purpose you will see your nature take on a whole new image. It will look more like the original image that we were made to reflect before the compulsion of living outside of that image took over. By willfully choosing to be what the Divine Being wants you to be you will reflect his character into the world through yours. As one of our favorite life scriptures says, "God intended that they would seek him and perhaps reach out for him and find him, though he is not far from each one of us. For in him we live and move and have our being." As some of your own poets have said, "we are his offspring." Therefore, being offspring of God, we should not think that the Divine Being is like gold or silver or stone an image formed by man's skill and imagination.

The way that you move, walk and talk will take on their most powerful form once you reconnect your being to his purpose. It is in him that you fully live, move and have your being. Not only will you see his reflection of purpose within your surroundings and circumstances, you will see his reflection in your soul, spirit and sight. Here is what we mean. To reflect his image you will see what you reflect *on* others even if you do not yet see his reflection *in* those you encounter. His image will cause you to look for his reflection in everyone and in everything which will have a profound impact on the flight of your life. You will look for him in the good and the bad, happy or sad, the highs and lows because you will understand that all of creation is on the same journey. So instead of seeing the enemy in everything, you will seek the inner *be* in everything.

If you feel that your connection with your higher purpose has been broken, there is good news. The way back is nearer to you than the distance you may have traveled or been taken away from. Just like the encounter between God and Moses you may need a deliverer who can take you and put you back on track to being all that you were created to be. God in his infinite being, has provided a Deliverer to reconnect you to the Source, *the goal*. You may recall that over the course of this book, we have been challenging you to respect and appreciate your goals but to never get them confused with *the goal*. *The goal* is, has always been and will forever be to get back to God. He is the giver of all life; he is the generator of altitude and lift. He is the Gracious Omnipotent Almighty Lord and the flight of your life is all about getting back to him.

He is *the goal* and every path points back to that truth. Every experience, every event, every teaching and every religion points back to the truth that we need God. However according to the scripture that we have used throughout the entirety of this book, there is only one way to reach *the goal*. That way is the Truth and the Life. The encounter between God and Moses was a reflection of how God would use one Redeemer to liberate anyone who wanted to be free. He can redeem your purpose and position you for propulsion. His name is Yasha, Yeshua, Iesu or most commonly, Jesus. The name we know him by literally means *to deliver*. That is the ultimate impact of propulsion. It is the purpose of propulsion. It is the goal of God. His desire is that we will all be delivered from the compulsive life that keeps us from living the propulsive life. He wants to ensure that we come to him safely, speedily and without damage, spot or blemish. The only one that has been entrusted to do this for him is his Son. Along the way his Son teaches us about his Father. He shows us the right way to do things and keeps us from the wrong way. He speaks to us and on behalf of us to his Father and converts all of your work into worship.

He puts us on the fast track to being all that we were made to be before we are scheduled for our final departure off this earth. If you have a relationship with him, in Him, all of your earthly goals will find completion and as he will prepare you for impact and pre-check you for eternity like TSA with Global Entry. In him you will find *meaning* beyond your achievements. You will find your *identity* beyond your work.

THE FLIGHT OF YOUR LIFE

You will be lifted up to a higher *class* of living. You will be *qualified* by his character. You will find your *belonging*. You will *live* with an intent and *objective*. You will find your *place* in life. You will be undisturbed in all things good or bad. You will see things *happen* for you and cause things to *occur* as you walk in his favor. You will finally know what it means to truly live and you will make an impact that goes deeper than the surface and into the soul.

LIVE IT

When I competed at the University of Mississippi my track-and-field coach said something, well many things, that impacted me. One day we happened upon a random discussion concerning champions. He said, "everyone notices a winner when they enter the room. A winner has something special, the 'X factor.' They may not always be the person who wins the championship but they walk, talk and move like they did. You can notice it in the way that they shake a hand and carry on a conversation. Everything about them says that they are a winner. They *live it* and you can feel it."

In every fiber of a winner's being is the secure self-declaration that "this is who *I am*." Those words have stuck with me for nearly twenty years and have been at the core of many of the successes, accomplishments, impressions and impacts I have had the honor of making. Winners live in this uninterrupted and undisturbed flow, knowing who they are. They live in a state of constant "*I am*." They live in a state of having already won. It is the difference between fighting *from* victory and fighting *for* victory. It is not "I will," "I want" or "I wish." It is "*I am*." They think, speak, train, compete, win and *learn* like a champion. Notice that I did not say *lose*. A champion never actually loses, they learn. Titles, belts or medals are only a reflection of their being. They are champions long before the recognition arrives or validates what they already knew. Winners are not pretending. They are actively engaged, intentionally living what they desire and generating the direction at every moment no matter what presents itself.

Likewise a great spouse does not instantly become a wonderful partner because they get married. Great spouses make decisions to be the type of mate they feel their spouse or significant other deserves even before they were in a relationship. They were setting healthy boundaries in their dating relationships and being conscious of how their actions will have pre-sent the man or woman they desired to be. A self-made multimillionaire does not just happen. These individuals possessed a million-dollar mindset or hustle mentality before they bought, sold or built a thing. They were actively listening, learning, growing and investing in assets and themselves until their income matched their input. Any well-known artist today was an artist before anyone gave them a deal or declared them to be one. They lived it when no one was looking or listening, when their only spotlight was the bathroom mirror, a school play or garage band.

Athletes that are now household names often share stories of how they would run, shoot, kick or throw something day and night. Each shot was the buzzer beater, every run was the game-winning touchdown and every sprint or throw earned the Olympic gold. Educators, authors, mechanics, doctors, lawyers, entrepreneurs, activists—you name it—lived their stories before they were ever told teaching, writing, repairing, helping, defending, building and standing up for the marginalized or often ignored. These are not coincidences, these are the results of choosing to *live* all that

THE FLIGHT OF YOUR LIFE

was prepared for them and that they were being prepared for. These individuals were prepared for impact and did not allow anyone to distract them from making it. Individuals who are determined to take the flight of their life have firmly established at some point, "this is who *I am*" and they will leave the rest of the world to deal with that weight.

The late Chadwick Boseman would often express how the words "this is who *I am*" influenced what roles he would accept and those he would decline. I can remember watching him recount the stories of particular agents who gave him roles that were stereotypical and did not reflect who he believed himself to be. He would say these agents would compel him to take a role because a particular director or actor was involved. His response would simply be "I want to work with *that* actor but I do not want to play *that* role. I want to meet that actor when I am doing something better than that." He continued to say, "because I said no at certain times, it made me available for the things that *got me to where I am*. For me it has always been first, who are you? Who am I? First. *I have to know who I am* first in order for me to know how to navigate this thing. *If I am navigating and I am becoming* something, if I become something that *I am not supposed to be*come then *I am* in the wrong place whether I 'made it' in the eyes of people or not." If Chadwick could not say, "this is who *I am*" then he did not take the role.

Remember that *I am* is the name of God as given to us by revelation knowledge. So in order to live the impact that you are being prepared for you must become one with the truth of the *I am*. When you become focused solely on living the truth of who *I am*, you will see an amazing shift in the atmospheres and environments that you will enter in and the impact that you will have on them. Focus on living all that *I am* has prepared you to be and the impact will come swiftly. This is why it is important that we come to know the *I am*, to protect the *I am* in ourselves and to always be observant of the *I am* in others.

    A mutual friend of ours Ro, reached out via text asking how we got into acting. I knew that his question contained more than what was presented so I gave him a call. Ro is a creative genius with a vivid childlike imagination. He creates comics and has a gift for illustration and cinematography. In his mind life happens on a set with multiple camera angles, full effects in cinematic detail and complete with a full soundtrack. One day Ro happened to see a trailer for a short film that I led in which prompted his question. I was amazed by his comments on the cinematography and the micro-expressions seen in my character. Wondering where this was heading, he began to share with me his childhood struggles as a student. He told me of how he excelled in all things creative as if it were his very own superpower.

    He expressed that no matter what he had done as an adult or where life had taken him, the only place that he truly felt free and fulfilled was when he was creating. Creative elements, sequencing and storytelling all came easily, naturally to him as a kid. Yet as happens to many of us and maybe even to you, living under compulsion led him to follow directions that pulled him away from who he felt that he was. My mind began picking up on his tonal inflections and I remember feeling the sorrow in his voice as if to say, "this is who *I am* but something happened that made me live differently."

    I remember Yvana and I visiting Ro in times past and no matter where he lived, he would always display his bat cave which was dedicated to all things creative: comic books, posters, superheroes, action figures and video games. He even had a full-sized Batman figure that guarded his creative fun zone. A few years back after visiting his new home, with his new wife and son, I noticed that he did not have any special sanctuary for these things. I did not think anything of it but Ro felt that he needed to tell me the story behind the disappearance of these items on this phone call.

A childhood friend had come to visit Ro. As usual he proudly displayed his treasure-filled bat cave. Unbeknownst to his guest, Ro was displaying far more than what he owned. As Ro displayed his signature room he was displaying scattered pieces of himself that reflected his nature but had not yet been identified as the connection between his purpose, passion and the impact that he was being prepared for. Unfortunately without a clear vision, it would not be long before the right challenge would cause him to question who he was becoming.

He shared the story of how a few carefully misplaced words tipped the scale knocking him out of the flow of what would be his *authentic identity*. As observed in the Pixar film *Soul*, these harmless words meant to give identity were enough to cause him to question who he *thought* he was. "I don't get it. You are a grown man and a minister with posters of superheroes on your walls, playing around with action figures. Doesn't the Bible say, '*when I was a child, I spoke as a child…but when I became a man, I put away childish things?*'" That was it. You may be thinking this should not have been all that was needed to take someone away from their purpose but think about your own life or the life of your loved ones or those who *could have been*. Often that is all that is necessary to shift us from living in confidence of the definitive "*I am*" to the insecure interrogative, "Am I?"

What could have made this experience different is simple. We have been discussing it throughout this book. You even read the examples of it in the opening paragraphs of the first chapter and at the beginning of this topic. It is the X factor that champions carry, the mindset that the wealthy possess. It is what connects your identity with the impact that you were prepared for. It is *vision*. Vision is what separates dreamers from the doers. All of the examples that we used before were meant to be examples of having one singular vision. Like Ro you may have a lot of passion, talent, giftedness, hope, faith and "creativeenius." Like his ability to illustrate, until there is a clear vision, the pieces will never come together and the story dies. *Where there is no vision the people perish*—that means you and the people you might propel prematurely.

Our encouragement is to take a look at all the pieces of you—everything that you want to be, were made to be and the impact that you were prepared for—and create a *vision statement*. This is very similar to a *positioning* statement but is a little different. A vision statement is your personal inspiration statement that defines your *ideal future, your existence*. It strengthens the positioning statement by declaring what you are trying to build with all of your pieces and serves as the absolute standard for your actions. A vision statement grounds you so that you can generate or actualize your existence and make the impact that you will have on the world a reality. You can always go back to your vision statement as your personal declaration of all that *"I am."* When you have found that you will find everything. *I am* encouraging you to live in the fullness of *I am* so that your potential, power, propulsion and prepared impact will be maximized and rooted in *all* that *I Am*.

GIVE IT

> *Give, and it will be given to you: good measure pressed down, shaken together and running over, will be poured into your lap. For the measure you use will be the measure you receive.*
>
> —Luke 6:38

THE FLIGHT OF YOUR LIFE

Everything that we have given to you up to this point has been meant to get you to this one. It is the one thought that will dictate whether you will actually take the flight of your life or accept a counterfeit, unfulfilled, striven version of it. This is the principle on which all of the other principles hang. It is the law that gives direction to all the other laws at play. In it lies the keys to the vehicle of your purpose and the power of propulsion. It is a very simple message with incredibly profound impact one that frees you to make the impact you were indeed, *in-deed*, prepared to make. It is the principle that separates the truly wealthy from those who only have an illusion of wealth.

This following principle speaks of those who have and exhibit the most *love*. It speaks of those who have and exhibit the most *joy*. It speaks of those who have and exhibit the most *peace*. It speaks of those who have and exhibit the most *patience* or forbearance. It speaks of those who have and exhibit the most *kindness*. It speaks of those who have and exhibit the most *goodness*. It speaks of those who have and exhibit the most *faithfulness*. It speaks of those who have and exhibit the most *gentleness* in force. It speaks of those who have and exhibit the most *self-control* or self-mastery.

This principle is a simple truth that often goes ignored or omitted. It is a divine law that despite the best of attempts to manipulate or to take advantage of, it can never be abolished. With all laws there are special stipulations written into their fabric. With divine laws the special stipulations are written into the fabric of existence, space and time. Whether you believe or are conscious or not, you are living within the parameters of these laws and may even be exercising them in your everyday life. You are mindful of these precepts even if you are not aware of their proper names. Law 1 is called *the law of reciprocity*. The second is *the law of sowing and reaping*. The third is the most important and it is most commonly known as *the law of Christ* which is often abbreviated into or boiled down to *the golden rule*.

The law of reciprocity is simple and like it, the law of sowing and reaping are siblings. The first says, "give, and it will be given to you." The second says, "whatever you sow, that you will reap." The third says to love God with all your heart, soul, mind and in conjunction to love your neighbor as you love yourself. The key to them all is the golden rule which is to *do to others as you would have them do to you*. These divine laws have been set up to propel anyone and everyone who observes them into the greatest impact and to offer a means to propel and to be propelled forward. They are set up in such a way that no one should feel compelled to do what they do not wish to. You may go as far or as fast as you are willing. You may give and sow as much or as little as you are willing. You do not have to get involved or give anything at all, it is entirely up to you. You are free to do nothing if this is the extent of the flight of your life.

You set the standards, measures and lengths that suit you and by doing so, you reciprocate the set of standards, measures or lengths that will be used for your return. This may sound familiar but if you recall our earlier discussion of the word *be*, you will comprehend that your be-ing ultimately determines your be-coming. The standard used to determine who, what, when, where and why of the magnitude of gift that you give, the pre-sent, determines the same of what you will receive in return. This can be applied to anything and everything. You cannot expect to take your game to the next level while giving the bare minimum effort, missing practice or just not giving a damn. You cannot expect to be heard without showing that you are willing to listen. You cannot expect to be trusted with much if you have not or are not being faithful with the little that you do have. Take an account of how much this principle applies to your current

THE FLIGHT OF YOUR LIFE

life and it will change the way you see what, how, to whom and to what purposes you are giving to.

If you expect to take the flight of your life but ignore others whose key you may be for their next level then you can expect doors to stay locked for you. If you are not giving of your time, talents or resources but are demanding that from others; if you are not giving your tolerance but demand acceptance; if you are not giving mercy and are cancelling or destroying others with your mouth or actions but demand mercy when you have offended and if you are denying or delaying justice for the voices who cry out against the years or livelihoods stolen from them but remain comfortable with lying, cheating, deceiving, or opening disputes for what does not belong to you, you should expect everything that you have coming. It does not matter what any of us believe that we deserve, these principles are preprogrammed to return to us exactly what we deserve. Even if the package is sent years ahead the return always comes—for our good or for our discipline. If you sow out of corruption or compulsion you will receive corrupted things. If you sow from a genuine place of propulsive purpose or to propel someone into purpose you will receive purposeful things.

Before we go we want to make this all make more sense to you. In each section of this book, we have emphasized a few key words in a progressive manner. We wanted your inner being to decode the message as if it were a radio transmission to you who was meant to read this right now. The words we are referencing are *passion*, *potential*, *power*, *propulsion* and *purpose*. Each of these topics depend on laws in order for their impact to *come to be*. The sequence of flight depends upon certain laws in order for flight to *occur*. We have taken a careful approach to the writing of this book by revealing the truth we have been trying to convey in a sequence that would prepare you for the impact that we wanted to make on you. The entire book can be summarized in this sentence: *passion* is the *potential* that initiates the *power* of *propulsion* which defines your purpose. We told you that we were going somewhere.

We could not just come out and say that to you from the beginning. One, we would not have had much of a book to read and two, there are so many layers, angles and truths to be explored in order to prepare how you viewed all of these things. We intentionally took the long route with layovers and pauses that would seemingly put one thought down and pick up another. We knew that we would need to carefully maneuver around passion points because starting with passion meant that we would need to create a separation in your thinking from the usual. We tried to remove you from the connotation that passion *is* your purpose. We hope now that you will see this book as a bit of a flight manual for the flight of your life. It does not cover every situation but the basics are enough to get you in the air and keep you and those who you will be entrusted with safe along the way to your making the impact that you were prepared to make.

This is the final piece to taking the flight of your life. If you can gather this principle above all else it will set your life on a course that is propelled at supernatural speed. You will no longer live under compulsion but above it and that will change how you lead, love and live. It will change how you approach the most obligatory of obligations as an opportunity to increase your propulsive position. Your money will increase, your expertise and worth will increase, your knowledge and wisdom will increase and your relationships and respect will increase.

> *passion* is the *potential* that initiates the *power* of *propulsion* which defines your purpose.

THE FLIGHT OF YOUR LIFE

There is nothing in your life that will be lacking if you decide to pursue these principles. You will see an immense amount of support, timing and resources open to you as you make the conscious decision to use all that you are to create paths to purpose for others using whatever means that you can. You will get yours and give that knowledge to others. You are not responsible for what they do with it but you are certainly reciprocated of what you give. It does not have to be free. That is not the last message we want you to misinterpret. It just needs to be made available. If you do this then you will find yourself on the flight of your life. Before you go take a look back into each topic and title. In them you will find a more complete understanding of what we mean regarding taking the flight of your life and how your life may look when you are actually on it. Each step of the way you were growing in clarity toward your dream. Follow our steps and we are sure that whatever you decide to achieve will have meaning and will ultimately lead you to make the impact that you were prepared to make:

Accept the call and choose to take action

Repent from past mistakes and misses

Pursue purpose above passion

Dare to defy the odds and do it scared

Remain seated in self-discipline and own it

Commit to rise above failed attempts along the way

Choose propulsive practices over compulsive patterns

Set healthy boundaries and keep right relationships

View responsibilities as a means for propulsive positioning

Use self-control in inner thoughts and self-talk

Listen carefully for rumblings that may indicate greater purpose

Increase impulses that increase your potential

Take time to strengthen and invest in areas where needed

Know how to hustle hard and when to recover harder

Live by universal laws and never local limitations

Use your gifts, talents, skills or abilities before they are lost

Do not allow circumstances to make excuses or make you quit

Be wise enough to know that potential can bring problems

Never compromise your latitude when climbing in altitude

Have a strong personal belief that you belong wherever you are

Keep others around who believe in you and themselves

Challenge the status quo and expect to endure times of testing

Learn how to use the skill of flight as your fight

Push the limits, limiters and limitations in your life

See your life as a business entity with you as CEO

Learn to say no to things that do not align with your brand of living

Recognize the present as a pre-sent investment you made the day before

THE FLIGHT OF YOUR LIFE

Use faith and wisdom to make actions that will propel your purpose

Be willing to do it alone if necessary and open to have others join you later

See the impact their life was created for and focus on making one

Use your power to generate change in others and convert them to believe

Pre-pair your resources for the be-coming before it arrives

Know the "I am" and walk in that way, truth and life in every endeavor

Live, build and store up in advance in preparation for what could be

Offer all that you are as a resource knowing that what you give will return

We hope that this book has taken you on an adventure that you may have not expected. We hope that you feel confident to do the work to maximize your potential for the purpose of maximizing that of others. We hope that you are inspired to use your resources to give all that you are and of all that you have learned. We hope that you have a new perspective of your qualification and a burning desire to give your entire being to the fullness of God.

Every lesson including the ones you are learning now, is the well from which you are qualified to draw. With these tools and insights we pray that you decide to repent, take action and live with intent and purpose. Whatever your determined destination we pray that you remain inspired and that you elevate everything around you. We hope that we have provided challenging insight into your greatest destiny. We have faith that you will come to see that your highest achievements will be found in the degree to which you deliver all that you were originally created to be so that others might find the courage to do the same.

Do not be surprised at the level of fun and freedom that you find in living these principles. We are inspired as we imagine the increase in your life that is coming. Profit much and propel others along the way. Live and leave a legacy of propulsion. Be the generator of hope, health, happiness and holiness in your generation. Push everything that is in you out into the world. Produce the book, produce the courses, produce the personal records, produce the KPIs and ROIs. There will be many who will follow your path. Continue moving forward, aspire higher and always set your mind on things above.

On behalf of Captain Charles, Captain Yvana and the entire crew, we would like to thank you for joining us on this trip. And we are looking forward to seeing you in the near future.

ABOUT THE AUTHORS

Charles and Yvana Bailey are visionary pioneers of propulsive purpose and emerging voices of aspirational empowerment. With their rich tapestry of experiences spanning professional athletics, corporate leadership, entrepreneurship, coaching and ministry, the Baileys have emerged as acclaimed trailblazers in the realm of personal and organizational growth.

Charles, a Master of Science and Executive Master of Business Administration (EMBA), a Certified Performance Coach and Actor brings a wealth of knowledge and experience. Meanwhile, Yvana, armed with a Master of Education and a Licensed Instructor and professional Model and Actor, channels her experiences on and off screen to instill confidence in her client's real life through one-to-one coaching and live seminars.

Together they offer a transformative approach to personal development that transcends traditional boundaries and ignites the flames of untapped potential. Their revolutionary signature programs, including Purpose Periodization®, Transcend Your Image® and Wake Up Woman™, stand as beacons of transformation empowering individuals and teams to shatter limitations, embrace authenticity and unleash their innate greatness upon the world.

But their impact extends far beyond the boardroom and playing field. Charles and Yvana are not just speakers. They are powerful and empowering storytellers, weaving narratives of resilience, redemption and remarkable triumph that resonate deep within the soul. Their dynamic keynotes, including *Push Your Limits*, *Take F.L.I.G.H.T.* and *The Potential Problem Paradigm*, transcend mere words—they are immersive experiences that stir the spirit, ignite passion and propel audiences toward their highest aspirations.

NEXT STEPS AND BONUS MATERIALS

As a token of appreciation for your support, purchasers of this book receive exclusive benefits, including complimentary access to a transformative 5 Days to Championship Level Confidence e-Course, valued at $249. Plus, a free 15-minute session with Charles or Yvana to kick-start your transformative journey which may be reserved at www.aspirehigherlife.com.

Please take a few minutes to show your support by giving a 5-star review and offer insight into what this transformative book has meant for you. We also encourage you to post your favorite quote in your review.

Subscribe to our free source podcast on YouTube, YouTube.com/@aspirehigherpodcast, or download our audio podcast on any major streaming platform for an ongoing wellspring of inspiration and insights to elevate your life and leadership. Join their thriving community of empowered individuals committed to scaling new heights of success, legacy and fulfillment.

Are you an event planner, leader or coach looking to elevate your team's performance, leadership and impact to unprecedented heights? Seize the opportunity to book

THE FLIGHT OF YOUR LIFE

Charles and/or Yvana Bailey for your next event, seminar or immersive experience. If you're in search of catalysts to usher in the transformative power of propulsive purpose take the first step toward securing Charles and Yvana to amplify your team or event's engagement, achievement and fulfillment.

The journey to greatness awaits—embrace it today.

BOOK BUYER'S BONUS:

15 MINUTES WITH COACH

Milton Keynes UK
Ingram Content Group UK Ltd.
UKHW022330050824
446508UK00013B/192/J